NATURAL RESOURCES AND THE ENVIRONMENT

*A Conference Sponsored by
the Changing Domestic Priorities Project
of The Urban Institute*

NATURAL RESOURCES AND THE ENVIRONMENT

The Reagan Approach

Edited by Paul R. Portney

The Changing Domestic Priorities Series
John L. Palmer and Isabel V. Sawhill, Editors

THE URBAN INSTITUTE PRESS · WASHINGTON, D.C.

Copyright © 1984
THE URBAN INSTITUTE
2100 M Street, N.W.
Washington, D.C. 20037

Library of Congress Cataloging in Publication Data
Main entry under title:

Natural resources and the environment.

(The Changing domestic priorities series)
Includes bibliographical references.
Contents: Introduction / Paul R. Portney—Natural resource policy / John D.
Leshy—Environmental policy / Robert W. Crandall and Paul R. Portney—[etc.]
1. Environmental policy—United States—Addresses, essays, lec-
tures.   2. Conservation of natural resources—United States—Addresses, essays,
lectures.   3. Energy policy—United States—Addresses, essays, lectures.
4. Agriculture and state—United States—Addresses, essays, lectures.   I. Portney,
Paul R.   II. Series.
HC110.E5N4   1984   363.7'056'0973   84-5276
ISBN 0-87766-334-3 (pbk.)
ISBN 0-87766-363-7 (cloth)

Printed in the United States of America

THE URBAN INSTITUTE is a nonprofit policy research and educational organization established in Washington, D.C. in 1968. Its staff investigates the social and economic problems confronting the nation and government policies and programs designed to alleviate such problems. The Institute disseminates significant findings of its research through the publications program of its Press. The Institute has two goals for work in each of its research areas: to help shape thinking about societal problems and efforts to solve them, and to improve government decisions and performance by providing better information and analytic tools.

Through work that ranges from broad conceptual studies to administrative and technical assistance, Institute researchers contribute to the stock of knowledge available to public officials and to private individuals and groups concerned with formulating and implementing more efficient and effective government policy.

Conclusions or opinions expressed in Institute publications are those of the authors and do not necessarily reflect the views of other staff members, officers or trustees of the Institute, advisory groups, or any organizations which provide financial support to the Institute.

THE CHANGING DOMESTIC PRIORITIES SERIES

Listed below are the titles available, or soon to be available, in the Changing Domestic Priorities Series

Books

THE REAGAN EXPERIMENT
An Examination of Economic and Social Policies under the Reagan Administration (1982), John L. Palmer and Isabel V. Sawhill, editors

HOUSING ASSISTANCE FOR OLDER AMERICANS
The Reagan Prescription (1982), James P. Zais, Raymond J. Struyk, and Thomas Thibodeau

MEDICAID IN THE REAGAN ERA
Federal Policy and State Choices (1982), Randall R. Bovbjerg and John Holahan

WAGE INFLATION
Prospects for Deceleration (1983), Wayne Vroman

OLDER AMERICANS IN THE REAGAN ERA
Impacts of Federal Policy Changes (1983), James R. Storey

FEDERAL HOUSING POLICY AT PRESIDENT REAGAN'S MIDTERM
(1983), Raymond J. Struyk, Neil Mayer, and John A. Tuccillo

STATE AND LOCAL FISCAL RELATIONS IN THE EARLY 1980s
(1983), Steven D. Gold

THE DEFICIT DILEMMA
Budget Policy in the Reagan Era (1983), Gregory B. Mills and John L. Palmer

HOUSING FINANCE
A Changing System in the Reagan Era (1983), John A. Tuccillo with John L. Goodman, Jr.

PUBLIC OPINION DURING THE REAGAN ADMINISTRATION
National Issues, Private Concerns (1983), John L. Goodman, Jr.

RELIEF OR REFORM?
Reagan's Regulatory Dilemma (1984), George C. Eads and Michael Fix

THE REAGAN RECORD
An Assessment of America's Changing Domestic Priorities (1984), John L. Palmer and Isabel V. Sawhill, editors (Ballinger Publishing Co.)

Advisory Board of the
Changing Domestic Priorities Project

Martin Anderson, Hoover Institution
John Brademas, President, New York University
Hale Champion, Executive Dean, John F. Kennedy School of
  Government, Harvard University
Nathan Glazer, Professor of Education and Sociology,
  Harvard University
Aileen C. Hernandez, Partner, Aileen C. Hernandez Associates
Carla A. Hills, Partner, Latham, Watkins & Hills (Chairman)
Juanita M. Kreps, Economist and former Secretary of Commerce
Thomas G. Moore, Hoover Institution
Richard F. Muth, Professor of Economics, Stanford University
Eleanor Holmes Norton, Professor of Law, Georgetown University
Paul H. O'Neill, Senior Vice President—Planning and Finance,
  International Paper Company
Peter G. Peterson, Chairman, Peterson, Jacobs and Company
Henry B. Schacht, Chairman, Cummins Engine Co., Inc.
Robert M. Solow, Professor of Economics, Massachusetts Institute of
  Technology
Herbert Stein, Professor of Economics, University of Virginia; Senior
  Fellow, American Enterprise Institute
Arnold Weber, President, University of Colorado
Daniel Yankelovich, Chairman, Yankelovich, Skelly and
  White, Inc.

CONTENTS

FOREWORD

In late 1981 The Urban Institute initiated a three-year project—Changing Domestic Priorities—to examine the shifts in domestic policy occurring under the Reagan administration and the consequences of those shifts. This volume, a product of the Changing Domestic Priorities project, is one of six collections of analyses by leading scholars on the impacts of current federal policies in a number of areas. The other five volumes are focused upon budget policy, economic growth, governance, regulatory policy, and social welfare policy.

Natural resource and environmental policy has grown more visible and controversial over the past decade, particularly when defined broadly enough to include actions affecting energy and agricultural markets. A decade and a half of new legislation has, in fact, reshaped the way our environment, energy supplies, agricultural lands, and other natural resources are used.

The Reagan administration took office with very different ideas about the way these resources should be managed—including the view that no federal presence was required in energy markets, and that a diminished government role was appropriate in managing the environment and other natural resources. Policies in each of these areas were rebalanced to place more emphasis on production and growth, on the one hand, and less on conservation and protection of resources, on the other.

The papers in this volume provide an assessment of these policies. They were first presented at a conference held in June 1983, sponsored by The Urban Institute and Resources for the Future.

In the first paper, Paul Portney provides an overview of the papers and identifies some similarities and differences between the administration's environmental, natural resource, energy, and agricultural policies. John Leshy assesses President Reagan's natural resource policies—those relevant to national parks and wilderness areas, on- and off-shore energy resources, endangered species and other wildlife, water supplies, and other valuable resources. Robert Crandall and Paul Portney examine the Environmental Protection Agency in the Reagan administration, and William Hogan focuses on the administration's energy policy. In the final paper, Bruce Gardner examines the agricultural policies pursued by the Reagan administration and their consequences.

We believe this volume, with its assessment of the controversies occurring since early 1981 and the changes those controversies have necessitated, will be of considerable interest to those who wish to understand the changing natural resources and environmental policy of this country.

John L. Palmer
Isabel V. Sawhill
Editors
Changing Domestic Priorities Series

INTRODUCTION

Paul R. Portney

President Reagan's proposed changes in domestic policies have been more controversial than any others offered since Franklin D. Roosevelt's first term. The controversy has embraced national defense and social welfare, taxing and spending policies and civil rights; but the most controversial intentions and actions of the Reagan administration have been those involving the nation's environmental and natural resources. These policies and actions, the source of almost constant squabbles between the administration and its critics, contributed largely to the all-but-forced resignations of the administrator of the Environmental Protection Agency (Anne M. Burford) and the secretary of the interior (James G. Watt).

This volume is the product of a conference held at the National Academy of Sciences in Washington, D.C., on June 6–7, 1983. The conference, sponsored by The Urban Institute and Resources for the Future, was organized around four commissioned papers that were later revised to form the present volume. Members of the academic community and other researchers attended, as did representatives of the environmental and business communities, of the executive and legislative branches of the federal government, of state and local governments, and of other organizations. In addition to the very helpful comments of two expert commentators assigned to each paper,[1] the authors

1. The commentators for John Leshy's paper were Marion Clawson of Resources for the Future and David Campbell of the National Wildlife Federation. J. Clarence Davies of the Conservation Foundation and John Quarles of Morgan, Lewis, and Bockius discussed the paper by Robert Crandall and Paul R. Portney. Joel Darmstadter of Resources for the Future and John Deutch of the Massachusetts Institute of Technology offered comments on William W. Hogan's paper. James Bonnen of Michigan State University and Lynn Daft of Schnittker Associates discussed the paper by Bruce Gardner. [The support of the Ford Foundation and the John D. and Catherine T. MacArthur Foundation is gratefully acknowledged.]

benefited from the sometimes lively discussion of their papers by the conference attendees.

Because this volume covers natural resource and environmental policy, it is concerned with the control of air and water pollution, toxic substances, pesticides, and hazardous wastes by the U.S. Environmental Protection Agency (EPA), and with the protection of endangered species, national parks, wildlife refuges and wilderness areas, and other publicly owned land managed by the U.S. Department of the Interior. Papers describing and analyzing the actions taken by the Reagan administration in the important, but somewhat less controversial, policy areas of energy and agriculture are also included. These areas must be included in any balanced assessment of the administration's treatment of the natural resources of the United States.

The Papers

John Leshy takes up the Reagan administration's management of the nation's public lands and water resources. He begins with the observation that the period between 1968 and 1980 saw virtually unprecedented changes in the size of the public estate. For example, the Alaska National Interest Lands Conservation Act doubled the size of the national park system and tripled the size of the national wilderness preservation and national wildlife refuge systems. These years also saw redefinition of the principles under which federally owned forests, rangelands, offshore oil and gas reserves, coal deposits, and other resources were managed. It is unlikely that any administration taking office in January 1981—Republican or Democratic, liberal or conservative—could have amassed a record of change comparable to that of the dozen or so preceding years. Thus, the proper baseline against which to compare the actions of the Reagan administration is not a simple extrapolation of pre-1981 policies. In certain areas, much less activism should have been expected of any administration.

Moreover, even with respect to the leasing of federal coal and offshore oil and gas rights, where the administration has claimed significant departures from the past,[2] the policies and procedures adopted in the late 1970s paved the way for expanded activity. Virtually any administration would have been more active in energy and mineral leasing than those occupying the White House during the 1970s (although the Reagan administration was indeed highly ambitious in this regard).

---

2. See U.S. Department of the Interior, "A Year of Progress: Preparing for the 21st Century," 1983.

Turning to policy on public lands and natural resources, Leshy notes that administrative reforms and budgetary initiatives have been the administration's favored instruments of change. Little effort has been devoted to changing the statutes that form the basis for the management of the public lands, even when key members of Congress shared the administration's views. By eschewing legislative change, the Reagan team runs the risk of having its administrative and budgetary initiatives overturned by its successors. Reluctance to work with Congress has even resulted in the immediate reversal of some of the administrative changes made at the Department of the Interior.

The administration's policies regarding water resources have been more sophisticated. Until recently, for example, the administration pushed for greater state and local sharing of the costs of new irrigation and navigation projects while continuing to fund projects now under way, particularly in the West. Leshy argues that, because of its high standing in the West, the Reagan administration is uniquely well positioned to reduce federal expenditures on water projects that fail to meet any reasonable benefit-cost test; the administration has so far shown little inclination to do so.

Following a discussion of federal timber, fish and wildlife, and grazing policies, Leshy turns to the least successful of the administration's initiatives—the so-called "privatization" of some public lands, and the attempt to allow mineral exploration and other commercial activities in wilderness areas. Reagan's attempt to sell federal lands identified as "surplus" by the Property Review Board he created should be viewed as distinct from Secretary Watt's apparently successful efforts to soothe the "sagebrush rebels" who supported Reagan's election. (According to Leshy, Watt virtually ended the sagebrush rebellion by reassuring westerners that state and local governments would have a greater say in the way federal lands were managed. Although very little land was actually returned to the control of lower levels of government, rumblings of western discontent quieted markedly.)

A very different fate befell the president's proposed sale of federal lands to private parties. This program, motivated by budgetary pressures as well as the doctrinal appeal of private ownership, encountered strenuous opposition from environmentalists, western governors and members of Congress, and from business interests who used the federal lands for grazing or to produce minerals or other commodities. This opposition derived in part from the many uncertainties surrounding the program: What role would Congress play in identifying or approving the sale of properties? Would state and local governments be given first crack at buying the lands? Would the interests of current users of the lands be protected? Coupled with an unwillingness to involve Congress in any aspect of the program (which was in marked contrast to the administration's acumen in negotiating the tax and budget cuts in 1981), these uncertainties spelled doom for the program, which has scarcely gotten off the ground.

The administration's efforts to open up certain wilderness areas to mineral exploration and extraction or other commercial activities have been even more controversial. Like the proposed sale of certain federal lands, these efforts were quickly and rather strenuously rebuffed by Congress, with opposition eventually coming even from western Republicans who might have been expected to support the proposal. Although Reagan's management of wilderness areas is far from a closed issue, it has not been a successful one in either a substantive or politically symbolic sense.

In Robert Crandall's and my chapter, we examine actions and policies at the EPA, concentrating primarily on the first two-and-a-half years of the Reagan administration. We begin by observing that this nation's efforts at environmental protection were encountering a number of serious problems before President Reagan took office—a point that has often been lost amidst the furor surrounding the agency's difficulties. But the point is important; it suggests that opportunities for constructive change in environmental policy did in fact await the new administration in January 1981.

The Reagan administration inherited problems of several sorts. First, there was a considerable number of standards whose issuance or revision was long overdue. The delays were threatening to undercut regulatory programs and heighten the uncertainty felt by regulated parties. The monitoring of existing ambient and discharge standards also left a great deal to be desired. Indeed, it was often difficult to tell which areas of the country were violating the ambient air quality standards and how serious these violations were; it was equally difficult to know which sources were contributing to the problems and in what proportions. Enforcement of the standards that had been issued was often inadequate. Moreover, the scientific basis on which a number of major EPA rules were based was often highly questionable. Coupled with the fact that EPA was forbidden to consider costs in setting certain important standards, this led to several regulations that appeared quite expensive relative to the uncertain benefits they provided. Finally, too little use had been made of economic incentives as tools of environmental policy in spite of impressive evidence that such tools could save money while still holding to the same or even higher levels of environmental quality.

To be fair to the pre-Reagan EPA, many of these shortcomings must be laid at the feet of a Congress prone to passing statutes with unrealistic goals and unreasonably short deadlines. These statutes are often based on a naive view of science and a disregard for the economic and other consequences associated with the pursuit of environmental quality. Yet even these statutory deficiencies posed an opportunity for the Reagan administration when it took office. One strong ground for critics of the Reagan EPA is its unwillingness to address and reform the problematical features of these fundamental statutes.

Other problems that arose at EPA during the first two-and-a-half years of the Reagan administration are better known. Many of these problems, including the allegations of incompetence or malfeasance that led to the mass resignations in early 1983,[3] can be traced to the inexperience of the initial appointees to the agency. This inexperience, and the appointees' unwillingness to rely on the EPA's career employees, boded ill for environmental policy. It also accounted, in the first months of the administration, for the lack of an agenda of possible changes to the environmental statutes. Once this early opportunity was missed, subsequent events at the agency made it impossible to regain.

Crandall and I also fault the Reagan administration for its actions regarding the EPA budget. Our concern is not so much with the overall budget reductions requested for the EPA, although a strong case could be made for augmenting rather than reducing the agency's total spending. The administration was probably justified in phasing out the noise control program, and was, in our view, too timid in reducing grants to states and local governments to subsidize the construction of sewage treatment plants. Rather, the administration should be faulted for reducing expenditures at the EPA in areas where more spending was clearly appropriate. Included in these are expenditures for research and development (particularly that dealing with the adverse health, ecological, and other effects associated with environmental hazards), and grants to the states to help them operate their ambient and source monitoring programs and conduct their enforcement efforts.

We conclude with recommendations for reform of environmental policy. These include budgetary changes of the sort suggested above as well as a sustained effort to expand the use of incentive-like mechanisms in environmental regulation. On the surface, the "new" EPA—the management team assembled by Administrator William Ruckelshaus and his deputy, Alvin Alm— would appear to be well suited to these tasks. Almost all of the new appointees have considerable experience in the areas for which they are responsible as well as an appreciation for the importance and sensitivity of their tasks. Moreover, their recent statements suggest a willingness to make better use of analysis in setting environmental standards and determining how standards might most efficiently be met.

In spite of the great capability of the new EPA, meaningful progress will be hard to make. First, the proximity of the 1984 presidential election and

---

3. In late 1983, Rita Lavelle (formerly assistant administrator for hazardous waste and emergency response) was convicted of perjury.

the budget deficit will dampen enthusiasm for all but the most cosmetic changes in environmental policy. In addition, it will be some time before the EPA will be free of the stigma earned by those appointed to the EPA in 1981.

Energy policy has been much less visible during the Reagan administration than during the three preceding ones. In William Hogan's paper, energy policy under Reagan is examined to see to what extent the relative quiet is due to the energy policies that the administration has pursued, and to what extent those policies were made possible by the diminished visibility of energy issues.

Hogan begins by pointing out that the first energy policy pronouncement of the administration—the early termination of remaining controls on domestic crude oil prices and allocation—was not only conceptually sound but also politically acute. The controls had made the energy crisis worse than it need have been, and removing them was consistent with the administration's free-market philosophy. Ending controls was also politically safe; declining demand and discord among OPEC producers suggested that world oil prices would soon be dropping. And drop they did.

The administration has taken a different tack with respect to natural gas regulation. Because there are many more potential "losers" from natural gas deregulation than from decontrol of oil prices, the administration has had to proceed more carefully. It sponsored legislation to accelerate the removal of price controls on "new" gas but it did not attempt the deregulation of "old" gas. In addition, the administration proposed a very un-laissez-faire-like step: the government-sanctioned abrogation of contracts between natural gas producers and pipeline companies. Although the administration's proposal has made little headway at this time, it is a considerable (and, Hogan implies, a sensible) departure from the total deregulation that candidate Reagan promised on the campaign trail.

Hogan is more critical of the Reagan administration's actions with regard to energy security, where the free-market approach is less relevant. Specifically, Hogan faults the administration for its initial reluctance to accelerate acquisitions for the Strategic Petroleum Reserve and an unwillingness to plan for possible future energy supply disruptions. The administration has, for example, been reluctant to push for an oil import tariff that would not only lessen dependence on foreign oil but would also bring in much-needed revenue.

Hogan is also critical of the administration's actions with respect to the budget of the U.S. Department of Energy. He is concerned about the overall level of funding, which he finds inadequate, as well as about the imbalance in the budget between nuclear power on the one hand and conservation and all other forms of energy supply on the other. In view of the doubtful economics of nuclear power, Hogan argues that this imbalance is inconsistent with the benefit-cost analysis that the administration is using elsewhere.

In the final paper, Bruce Gardner discusses agricultural policy in the Reagan administration. Although less controversial than the policies made at the EPA or the Department of the Interior, agricultural policy has come under close scrutiny of late because of the skyrocketing costs of the program the administration conceived to assist farmers. Nevertheless, as in energy policy, there are respects in which the administration's initiatives have made some sense.

Because low farm incomes are often advanced as a reason for government intervention, Gardner begins his analysis by reviewing the general financial condition of the farm sector. Contrary to popular opinion, he finds that in spite of a decline in 1982 from 1980 and 1981 levels, real income per farm family was 50 percent higher in 1982 than it was in 1960, while the average net worth of a farm had increased 150 percent. The top 25 percent of all farms in terms of sales (which account for 88 percent of total farm sales) did even better—the average net worth of these enterprises was $531,000 in 1980. Thus, although financial problems plague certain farms, depressed farm incomes are an insufficient basis for the general shape of current agricultural policy. The other frequently cited justification for federal intervention, price instability, is also unconvincing, particularly because intervention is often used to protect farm incomes rather than to smooth price movements.

Turning to actual policy, Gardner concludes that the administration's initial intentions were quite sound. These included a 1981 freeze on milk support prices and a stated intention to phase out target prices and deficiency payments for grains and cotton. However, when the basic law governing agricultural policy was rewritten in 1981, the administration failed to secure these or other changes. The Agriculture and Food Act of 1981 increased the real support prices for corn and wheat by 10 percent and 5 percent, respectively (contrasted with declines of 9 percent and 3 percent, respectively, between 1977 and 1980), although the increases might have been even larger had the administration not tried to keep them down. In its unwillingness to fight for more fundamental changes in the Agriculture and Food Act of 1981, the administration followed a pattern established in the environmental and natural resource areas—it relied on administrative discretion rather than legislative action as the major instrument of policy change.

The most important element in the Reagan administration's agricultural program is the Payment in Kind (PIK) program. This program was intended to accomplish two goals: protect farm incomes and reduce the drain on the federal budget caused by the government's having to buy and store grains. The PIK program allowed farmers participating in a pre-existing acreage reduction program to idle still more land in exchange for in-kind payments (from government stocks) of the crops they would not be producing. The acreage reductions were intended to drive prices up, and so reduce government support payments, while lowering storage costs by reducing government-held stocks.

According to Gardner, this program resulted in the largest acreage diversion in U.S. history in 1982—82 million acres, greater by 28 percent than the highest previous year. A precise evaluation of PIK is difficult; but after carefully tracing the program's effects on one commodity, corn, Gardner concludes that the PIK program was not very successful. For this one commodity alone, the PIK program appears to have cost U.S. taxpayers and consumers $1 billion more than the benefits it provided to participating corn growers in 1983. In addition, the idling of land adversely affected sellers of farm equipment, fertilizers, and other items used in agriculture.

In spite of his generally pessimistic evaluation of the realized effects of the PIK program, Gardner credits the administration with a willingness to innovate in agricultural policy. He expresses the hope that this willingness to experiment will be extended to possible deregulation of some commodity prices. Although this is apparently consistent with the administration's principles, it would no doubt result in the kind of legislative battle that the administration has been reluctant to fight.

Common and Contrasting Themes

Although there are similarities in the Reagan administration's conduct of energy, environmental, agricultural, and natural resource policies, there are also differences. It may be worthwhile to emphasize the latter to avoid the facile impression that these policies can be taken as a piece.

First, although criticism of the Reagan administration's energy and agricultural policies has sometimes been sharp, it has usually focused on the substance of policy rather than on its conduct. That has not been true for environmental and natural resource policies; there, the personalities of those formerly in charge of policy—Anne M. Burford at the EPA and James G. Watt at the Department of the Interior—were as much at issue as the policies themselves. Ultimately, the perceived vindictiveness or incompetence with which these policies were pursued led to the replacement of both officials with more seasoned and less controversial appointees.

Second, as judged by the administration's announced intentions, its success in these four policy areas has varied. For example, the Department of

Energy still exists (contrary to the President's pledge to abolish it), but the administration has had some success in energy policy. Reagan made good on his promise to accelerate the decontrol of crude oil and gasoline prices and was seen to be successful in doing so. Moreover, the administration succeeded in substantially altering the composition of the department's budget, moving emphasis away from solar and conservation initiatives and toward nuclear programs.

In spite of the controversy surrounding Secretary Watt, and a number of notable reversals at the hands of Congress, the administration has had some success at the Department of the Interior. For example, there has been a substantial increase in the amount of federally-owned coal that has been leased, as well as an increase in outer continental shelf acreage leased for oil and gas exploration. Some much-needed reform of the cost-sharing arrangements concerning federally-sponsored water projects was introduced (but later hedged upon). And the restiveness of the western states about the federal ownership and management of much of their land seems at least temporarily stilled. These accomplishments must be weighed against the very considerable difficulties that have arisen concerning the conduct of natural resource policy at Interior.

Even when weighed against their own goals, however, there are fewer successes to recount in environmental or agricultural policy in the Reagan administration. An administration espousing a free-market approach to agriculture has become the custodian of the greatest land diversion program in history. Moreover, federal payments to farmers have risen from about $3 billion in 1980 to nearly $19 billion for 1983, hardly an extrication of the government from agricultural production.

Problems at the EPA have been even more pronounced. Apart from accomplishing the goal of cutting the agency's budget (which could only frustrate other of the administration's stated goals), virtually nothing went right at the EPA until the across-the-board changes in management in mid-1983. Little progress was made in furthering the use of economic incentives as tools of environmental policy, and what was accomplished owed more to the career staff inherited from the Carter administration than to Reagan appointees. The management of the politically sensitive Superfund program, which deals with the cleanup of abandoned hazardous waste disposal sites, was badly botched; "hit lists" of politically unacceptable science advisors and career employees were prepared and acted upon; and public confidence ebbed in the administration's resolve to monitor pollution problems carefully and pursue violators rigorously. In spite of substantial recent improvement, environmental policy is surely the administration's least successful area.

The Reagan administration's policies regarding the environment, energy, agriculture and natural resources have some important similarities, the most notable of which is a reliance on administrative discretion rather than on legislative change as the preferred instrument of policy redirection. Indeed, the administration has eschewed effort at legislative change in all but a few cases, even when very promising opportunities appeared.

For example, no effort was made to amend the Mining Law of 1872, which governs mineral exploration and development, although key members of Congress of both parties seemed to share the administration's view of the changes needed in the law. Similarly, no meaningful effort was made to amend the Clean Air Act although it is the most important federal regulatory statute, and in spite of the fact that several proposed revisions were offered in 1981 and 1982 by members of Congress with views close to those of the Reagan administration. The administration made no real effort to rewrite the Food and Agriculture Act of 1981, either, although it is the fundamental statute under which agricultural policy is conducted in the United States. Nor has the administration yet launched an all-out effort to win repeal of existing price controls on natural gas, in spite of a campaign promise to do so. (Decontrol of crude oil price and allocation was accomplished administratively rather than legislatively.)

There are probably a number of reasons for this legislative reluctance. It is always more difficult to push legislation through Congress, especially when one house is controlled by the opposite party, than it is to alter policy through administrative fiat. This is all the more true when the proposed changes are drastic ones. The administration may also have suffered from exhaustion after pushing through Congress the multiyear tax cuts it won in 1981 and the expenditure cuts it proposed for that and subsequent years. Given the administration's relative lack of interest in the environment and natural resources, legislative battles may not have seemed worth the effort.

There is a price to pay for inattention to legislative change, however; subsequent administrations can more easily reverse policies pursued through administrative action alone. Fundamental change is much more likely if an administration takes the time to work closely with Congress in redirecting policy. It is unlikely, therefore, that in ten years the Reagan administration will be seen as one that fundamentally altered the course of natural resource policy.

Another element common to administration policy in these four areas is the gap between what was promised and what has been delivered. To be sure, all new administrations enter with grand visions of what will be done and leave pointing proudly to much lesser accomplishments; but in many ways the Reagan administration outdid its predecessors in the extravagance of its claims. The Department of Energy was to be abolished; the government was to end its involvement in agriculture; public lands and wilderness areas were to be opened up for energy and mineral exploration and production; and environmental policy was to be streamlined and more use was to be made of economic approaches to pollution control and environmental enhancement.

Nearly four years later, the Department of Energy has its second secretary and is actively helping to formulate administration policy concerning the deregulation of natural gas, planning for emergency interruptions of imported oil, and participating in many other important functions. The government is now much more—not less—involved in agriculture and is looking hard for ways to lessen that involvement; no one is talking very loudly about getting out altogether. In spite of (or perhaps because of) Secretary Watt's bombastic rhetoric, very little has been done to open up heretofore unavailable lands for more commodity production. (John Leshy argues that it may now be more difficult than ever before to open these lands because of the adverse public and congressional reaction to policies originating in the Department of the Interior.) Finally, environmental policy is only now beginning to move ahead sensibly, following two-and-a-half years of near chaos. Even carefully considered policies to promote the use of economic incentives in environmental protection will face a much tougher reception now than they would have four years ago because of the ill will engendered by the original appointees to the EPA.

Similarities and differences are detailed in the following chapters. Recent changes in policies and management at the EPA and the Department of the Interior may put an end to criticisms of environmental and natural resource policies in Reagan's first term. If so, they will surely make it easier for him to run a second time.

NATURAL RESOURCE POLICY

John D. Leshy

When President Reagan took office he intended, as he put it, nothing less than to set the nation on a fundamentally different course. The administration's objectives included limiting domestic federal spending, reducing the regulatory burden on private industry, transferring responsibilities to state and local governments as part of a new federalism, and relying more on the private sector and market mechanisms for fulfilling social goals. Each of these is readily applicable to federal natural resource policies, where the federal presence in both spending and regulation has been growing, where federal displacement of state and local governmental functions has been increasingly debated, and where the private sector has chafed under increasing federal restrictions. Natural resources policy, then, presented the Reagan administration with an ideal setting in which to translate its vision into reality.

Of course no administration can pursue its policy objectives in a vacuum—transitory political considerations inevitably hamper the translation of goals into achievements. But this administration came to office dedicated more strongly than most to its chosen tenets, headed by a president who not only commanded considerable personal popularity and communication skills, but also almost uniformly appointed like-minded persons to key positions. Thus its record in applying these tenets is worth considerable scrutiny. The most notable feature of Reagan's natural resource policies is not the clarity with which the administration expresses its goals, but the highly selective way in which it implements them, and the skill (or lack of it) with which it has resolved conflicts among its objectives.

Background

No administration assuming office in January 1981 could have ignored the far-reaching changes in federal natural resource policies fashioned in the

13

previous twelve years. Scarcely a month after Ronald Reagan was elected president, Congress wrapped up nearly a dozen years' labor by enacting legislation charting the future management of more than 100 million acres of federal land in Alaska. Perhaps the most significant natural resource legislation of this century, the Alaska National Interest Lands Conservation Act was an appropriate capstone to a remarkably activist era.

Although any demarcation of such an era is somewhat arbitrary, this one might conveniently be bounded by the national debate over management of the resource-rich Alaska lands that began in the waning days of the Johnson administration. The following years saw federal natural resource policies change at a pace and with a scope unparalleled since the turn of the twentieth century. Nearly all resources—lands, oceans, minerals, wildlife, timber— were affected as the nation grappled with now-familiar issues of preservation, exploitation, and environmental regulation.

Applying to nearly all federal actions affecting the environment, the National Environmental Policy Act of 1969 (NEPA) had more thorough effects on federal natural resource policy than anywhere else. Along with related requirements written into new laws for public participation and openness in governmental decisionmaking, the NEPA subjected federal natural resource policymaking and implementation to public and judicial scrutiny as never before. Another landmark act of those years was the Surface Mining Control and Reclamation Act of 1977, which created a federally supervised environmental protection program for coal mining throughout the nation. The act capped nearly three decades of congressional effort and survived two presidential vetoes.

In other efforts, legislative and administrative action were combined to reform the programs for developing federal coal onshore and oil and gas deposits offshore; new legislation (e.g., the Fishery Conservation and Management Act, the Coastal Zone Management Act, the Marine Sanctuaries Act and the Marine Mammal Protection Act) expanded regulatory control over ocean-related resources; public lands managed by the Bureau of Land Management (BLM) were given their first comprehensive charter in the Federal Land Policy and Management Act; and two acts overhauled management of the national forests. Congress also provided strong federal protection for endangered species, archeological resources, and historic sites and artifacts, and added significant acreage in the lower forty-eight states to the national park, wildlife refuge, wilderness, and wild and scenic rivers systems. The Alaska lands legislation by itself tripled the size of the national wilderness preservation system and the national wildlife refuge system, doubled the size of the national park system, added twenty-four rivers to the national wild and scenic rivers system and 3 million acres to the national forest system. All told, these efforts were so comprehensive that enactment of the Alaska legislation seemed nearly to exhaust the national natural resources agenda.

Just as many observers saw President Johnson's Great Society as a second phase of the New Deal, so the years 1968 to 1980 might be viewed as an outgrowth of the conservation movement that flowered between 1900 and 1920. The philosophical ties to the earlier movement are not always distinct; for example, much greater emphasis was placed on preservation and environmental quality in the modern era.[1] But in general, the guiding principle of both eras was the felt necessity of subjecting the private exploitation of land and other resources to more governmental control.

Conflict between the executive and legislative branches also appeared in both eras; but where the earlier movement saw the executive branch seize the initiative and lead an often reluctant Congress to follow, its modern counterpart saw Congress play a more aggressive role, sometimes leading or overruling a less enthusiastic executive. Between 1900 and 1920 Congress for the most part delegated broad authority to (or acquiesced in the assumption of authority by) the executive branch, but even a casual glance at the legislation enacted between 1968 and 1980 shows that the modern Congress sought to recapture some of this authority. It engaged in the details of natural resource policy making and program administration much more fully, often legislating remarkably specific environmental performance standards, decision making procedures, and the like. Executive discretion, while still considerable, has been significantly narrowed; moreover, it is now subject to much more review from outside the executive branch (especially by means of public participation and judicial review) than was common in the earlier era.

A few areas of natural resource policy making remained substantially unchanged, if not free from controversy—federal water policy, for example. But passage of the Alaska legislation seemed to signal the end of the modern activist era. Admittedly, it is not easy to distinguish the apparent shift in national mood, as reflected in the 1980 election, from the waning of reform efforts in natural resource policy; thus final enactment of the Alaska legislation in the lame-duck session was unmistakably influenced by that election. Even a second Carter administration, however, might well have left a mark on natural resource policy quite unlike those of the administrations before it.

The comprehensiveness of these recent policy changes suggests an obvious difficulty in comparing the Reagan administration's record with those of its predecessors. Because few areas of policy making remained untouched by reform efforts, and because these reforms settled (or appeared to settle)

---

1. See, e.g., Robert H. Nelson, "The Public Lands," in P. Portney, ed., *Current Issues in National Resource Policy* (Washington, D.C.: Resources for the Future, 1982), pp. 28–32.

so many fundamental natural resources management controversies, the new administration had fewer opportunities to contribute to the resolution of outstanding issues. Comparing, for example, the amount of acreage added to, or the amount of dollars spent on, the park, refuge, or wilderness systems in 1981 and 1982 with the additions or expenditures of any two of the preceding twelve years would be fundamentally misleading.

Significantly, however, the Reagan administration has chosen to dwell on such comparisons in the important area of federal mineral development. Former Secretary of the Interior Watt's second annual report[2] opened with a wealth of data showing the great acceleration of onshore and offshore federal energy leasing. But such statistical comparisons are largely empty of meaning. The Nixon administration placed a moratorium on federal coal leasing in 1971, and the new coal leasing system unveiled a few years later was enjoined by the courts. Congress meanwhile passed the 1976 Federal Coal Leasing Amendments and, less than a year later, the Surface Mining Control and Reclamation Act. It was not until 1980 that a program that incorporated these new requirements and was generally acceptable to all major interests—state and local governments, industry, environmental groups, and ranchers—was finally installed. Thus the Reagan administration found itself to be the first administration in ten years that was in a position to engage in substantial coal leasing. Federal coal leasing was bound to have increased sharply after 1981 simply because all the pieces had finally been put in place.

The Reagan administration benefited in much the same way in oil and gas leasing. The offshore oil and gas leasing program had gone through an upheaval similar to that in coal in the 1970s. With implementation of new legislative reforms and the opening of frontier areas along the east, west, and Alaskan coasts, Carter's Secretary of the Interior Andrus had proposed in 1980 to double outer continental shelf leasing over the next five years. Meanwhile, allegations of fraud in onshore leasing had led to a temporary moratorium on that program, and the huge onshore naval petroleum reserve in northern Alaska was not opened to leasing by Congress until 1978, and it took two years to promulgate the necessary regulations and establish the leasing capability for this brand-new program.

This is not to argue that the Reagan administration has not done things differently from what President Carter, if reelected, or another president would have done. It should, however, underscore the fact that policy changes cannot be identified or measured by statistics alone. Because the Reagan administration was in a position to capitalize immediately on the work of earlier

---

2. *1982—A Year of Progress: Preparing for the 21st Century* (Washington, D.C.: U.S. Department of the Interior, 1982).

years, such statistics may indeed be downright misleading when used to compare its policies to other administrations.

The pace of reform between 1968 and 1980 could not have been sustained. Any new administration could have been expected to pause, to concentrate on the less visible but important task of consolidating and assimilating these changes into the day-to-day task of governing the nation's natural resources. But the Reagan administration's agenda was more ambitious: to reconsider and modify many of the recent reforms. "I am a sagebrush rebel," candidate Reagan announced, neatly capturing in that phrase a discontent with those reforms shared by widely disparate interests. Significantly, although Watt's first annual report set out the seemingly noncontroversial goals of restoring "common sense" and "balance" in natural resource policy making, these words were intended and understood as a code for changing existing policies, not just the manner of their implementation.

The Administration and Legislative Reforms

Given its ambitious objective, this administration had to decide at the outset the extent to which it would seek to involve Congress in its program. This was an especially sensitive issue because so many of the reforms of the previous decade were embodied in detailed legislation. Change would thus be difficult without the concurrence, or at least the acquiescence, of Congress.

The administration appeared to make this crucial decision without difficulty. For all of its ambitious rhetoric, the administration decided early on not to submit any major natural resources legislative proposals to Congress (other than appropriations). This failure to enlist congressional assistance is the more remarkable because the president helped sweep the Republicans into power in the Senate where Senator McClure, a staunch supporter of the Reagan program, was assuming control of the key Energy and Natural Resources Committee.

It was not immediately clear whether the administration's unwillingness to push for legislation was motivated by its judgment (contrary to its campaign rhetoric) that the recent reforms for the most part were adequate and sensible, or by the realization that the political climate was not ripe for their undoing, especially with the Democrats still in control of the House. The transition report[3] that furnished most of the administration's early policy initiatives recommended pursuit of several legislative rollbacks, and there were persistent rumors in the first eighteen months of the administration that major amend-

---

3. Robert L. Terrell and David C. Russell, *Mandate for Leadership: Project Team Report for the Department of the Interior* (Washington, D.C.: Heritage Foundation, 1980).

ments to recently enacted legislation were being drafted. Almost none of these ever saw the light of day, however, and eventually the administration's chief spokesman on natural resources, Secretary Watt, started singing a strikingly different tune. He began, for example, to describe the coal surface mining act—repeatedly singled out during the 1980 campaign as an example of environmental protectionist excess—as a fundamentally good and workable law.

Furthermore, when Congress has addressed substantive legislative issues, the administration has shied away from the legislative process, and even accepted without serious protest legislative amendments reversing reforms that it had previously adopted administratively. It seems likely that policy changes will remain almost wholly administrative rather than legislative, and that the administration will be highly selective in choosing issues for legislative battles.

Undoubtedly a major factor in the administration's early legislative timidity was its reluctance to divert energy from the budgetary reforms that occupied center stage in the 97th Congress. That effort is no longer dominant, but in the natural resources area the timidity persists. The administration's unilateral initiatives (and the personalities with which they have been identified), may have reinforced a mutual distrust between the legislative and executive branches that transcends party affiliations.

Natural Resource Budgeting

The administration has necessarily depended on Congress in one important area—appropriations. Here the administration has moved aggressively, revealing its policy priorities by pushing for deep reductions in several program areas and substantial increases in others.

The administration's basic objective of reducing the size of federal domestic programs has been carried out with vigor in many areas of natural resource policy. Three agencies—the Water Resources Council (and the Regional River Basin Commissions that operated under it), the Office of Water Resources and Technology, and the Heritage Conservation and Recreation Service—have been abolished; the first two outright, with some of the last's functions shifted to the National Park Service. The administration has also tried to eliminate the Land and Water Conservation Fund, through which federal, state, and local governments acquire land for parks and recreation areas with revenues from federal offshore oil and gas leasing. Although this effort has not wholly succeeded, actual appropriations from this fund have been dramatically reduced by Congress. The administration has, however, undertaken a five-year Park Rehabilitation and Improvement Program that is estimated to cost about the same amount. It has, in short, shifted emphasis sharply from increasing the supply of park and recreation land at all levels of government to providing more funds for existing federal parks.

The outcome of the administration's battle with Congress over the Land and Water Conservation Fund typifies most of the budget battles in the natural resources area: the administration has not carried the day entirely, but its proposals to eliminate or deeply cut targeted programs have usually resulted in significant reductions. Besides land acquisition, affected areas include federal trail maintenance, wildlife habitat protection, resource inventories, planning, environmental studies, regulatory enforcement, and various fish, wildlife, and recreation grant programs.

The administration's approach to appropriations for national forest management is particularly revealing, for that is one area where benchmark budget projections are readily available. The congressionally mandated five-year plan adopted by the Carter administration in 1980 established budgetary goals by category of use. The current administration's emphasis shows clearly in its departures from these goals—funds for timber and minerals production have been fully protected or even increased, while funds for wildlife, recreation, and soil and water protection have been significantly reduced.

As this illustrates, the administration's budgetary tilt is sharply away from the "softer" areas of recreation, preservation, and environmental protection and toward the more traditional, "harder" or commodity uses of natural resources. Thus, amid the budget-cutting fervor, two areas have survived the administration's red pencil rather well indeed—federal water project construction and mineral development programs. The administration's approach to water project funding has not, however, been fully consistent; the administration has generally protected funding for Bureau of Reclamation projects in the West, while it has sought to reduce the Soil Conservation Service's small watershed program and to collect user fees to pay for harbor and inland waterway improvements undertaken by the Corps of Engineers. Other budget reduction proposals have been sacrificed to political prudence; for example, a proposal to require federal permits with accompanying fees for hunting and fishing on federal lands was withdrawn four days after submission to Congress.

The administration's budget-paring sentiments have elsewhere plainly outweighed its intentions to resuscitate federalism. Unlike onshore mineral leasing, where states are allowed to tax federal mineral production and where most federal revenues are funneled back to these states, Congress has never directly shared revenues from the far more lucrative outer continental shelf leasing program with the affected coastal states. Congress is again seriously considering such a proposal (one passed the House in 1982 but died in the Senate). In the face of the administration's sharp expansion of outer continental shelf leasing and its budget cuts in other coastal-related, environmentally oriented programs, this legislation has attracted support from the oil and gas industry and environmentalists as well as the coastal states. But the administration has steadfastly opposed offshore revenue sharing, although it has proposed no significant alteration in onshore mineral revenue distribution. Like federal reclamation water projects, onshore mineral leasing revenue benefits the Republican heartland states, and the budgetary policies of this administration have been heavily colored by such conventional political considerations.

Federalism in Natural Resources Management

Another goal of the administration's program is to strengthen federalism or, more pointedly, to lessen the burdens of a growing, domineering federal presence. But the political safeguards associated with federalism actually operated quite effectively in the remarkable sweep of federal natural resources legislation between 1968 and 1980. In many cases the states' position vis-a-vis the federal government was actually bolstered. Some strengthening was purely financial; for example, the 1976 Payments in Lieu of Taxes Act and Congress' creation that same year of a more generous formula for sharing federal onshore mineral leasing revenues with the states. Other legislation required federal activities to be as consistent as possible with state and local government land use policies; for example, the Coastal Zone Management Act and, to a somewhat lesser extent, the Federal Land Policy and Management Act. Further, when Congress widened opportunities for public participation in federal decision making, state and local governments were almost always singled out for special, favorable treatment. And even where Congress did create new federal requirements that overrode less stringent state ones, as in the Surface Mining Control and Reclamation Act, it followed the now-familiar practice of inviting the states to take over the regulatory function and providing financial and other inducements to encourage them to do so. Finally, previous administrations had shown some sensitivity to these concerns; for example, the Carter administration's coal leasing program was largely designed to improve the ability of affected states to guide the timing, location, and amount of federal coal to be leased.

Thus, even with all this federal activity, the interests of state and local governments were usually well protected; indeed, it could be said that the tide was actually running in their favor. Nevertheless, candidate Reagan, waving the banner of the sagebrush rebellion, managed to reap considerable political advantage from the alleged federal insensitivity to state concerns. That campaign rhetoric has occasionally come back to haunt his administration as it wrestles with conflicts between states' rights and federal budgetary and resource development decisions.

Summary

The administration's strong preference for budgetary manipulation and administrative reform, rather than substantive change in existing laws, has had a number of consequences. By not seeking statutory change, this administration is allowing its policy changes to be more easily undone by future ones. This exacerbates the "moving target" problem faced by affected states and private firms, for their budgetary and investment decisions are best made against a relatively stable federal policy. Further, implementing reforms without overt congressional endorsement has meant pushing executive power to limits rarely seen since the days of Theodore Roosevelt, and this also has its costs. Most obviously, the administration has courted conflict with a Congress increasingly accustomed to asserting itself in natural resource policy making. The result is that the administration has tended to isolate itself politically, allowing attention to its policies to center on the strident personality of former Secretary Watt.

This is not, in short, an administration that has generally sought to develop consensus policies in natural resource management. Rather, it has gone its own way, aggressively exercising whatever discretion Congress has given it in pursuit of its own goals, and relying heavily on the personal popularity of the president and the difficulty Congress always has in acting affirmatively to block executive actions.

From a broader perspective, there has been a remarkable inconsistency between this administration's rhetoric and its actions—the rhetoric being couched in terms of launching revolutionary reform in natural resources policies, and the actions being confined almost wholly to budgetary recommendations and administrative decisions. But truly fundamental reform remains impossible without congressional cooperation. The administration has thus boxed itself in; by pursuing administrative reforms with such vigor, it has become alienated from Congress to such a degree that cooperation will not readily be forthcoming.

Substantive Policy Changes

The Reagan administration has proposed policy changes in all major substantive areas of federal natural resource policy. This section offers a review of some of the more important or illustrative of such changes. Two special initiatives, opening wilderness areas to mineral development and "privatizing" federal lands, are treated separately below.

Hardrock Minerals

The early days of the Reagan administration saw the end of a long-standing effort to repeal the law governing hardrock mining on federal lands, the Mining Law of 1872. The effort was already moribund; President Carter's call for reform, echoing proposals from previous administrations, had fallen on deaf ears on Capitol Hill. In a clean break from both the Ford and Nixon administrations, as well as Carter's, the Reagan administration pledged to clear away obstacles to more hardrock mining on federal lands.

So far, however, this strong rhetorical support has not been translated into action. It is curious that the administration has not seized a clear legislative opportunity to achieve reform here. The Mining Law is inadequate from nearly all vantage points, including industry's, for it contains various archaic limitations that severely hamper mineral exploration and development on a modern scale. Although industry supporters in Congress have been nurturing legislative reforms that seemed to comport generally with the administration's policy goals, there has been no executive support for this effort and it has so far languished.

The major claim of the administration here is an empty one—that it has issued "the most powerful Presidential statement on national minerals policy in nearly three decades."[4] Although there can be no denying this—actually it was only the second such statement in history—there is also no denying the fact that under the statement's rhetoric was comparatively little substance. The domestic minerals industry, which had much higher expectations, was bitterly, if quietly, disappointed.

There may be more action in the near future, for the Department of the Interior is considering administrative reforms in the Mining Law. A general effort to simplify the transfer of federal property rights to private mining claimants, long sought by the mining industry, seems likely. But the antiquated law may not support such tinkering, and it will be difficult to exclude from this process issues that the industry would prefer to leave undisturbed, such as environmental protection standards. It is characteristic that the emphasis remains on administrative rather than legislative reforms.

Ironically, the Reagan administration has taken some steps that may actually undermine solutions to the United States' dependence on certain

---

4. See note 2. See also *National Materials and Minerals Plan and Report to Congress* (Washington, D.C.: Executive Office of the President, 1982).

imported strategic minerals. For budgetary reasons, it has cut research and development support for minerals and materials processing, substitution, and recycling, and has given little attention to stockpile expansion, emphasizing instead greater exploration of federal lands. This tactic is of dubious effectiveness, given five to twenty year lead times for production, and it has exacerbated concern about wilderness protection.[5]

Mineral Leasing. The Reagan administration has placed a high priority on accelerating the transfer of federal energy minerals to the private sector.[6] Three things have allowed the administration to make considerable headway here. First, Congress has always accorded the Secretary of the Interior a great deal of discretion in deciding when and where to issue federal mineral leases; even the reforms of the 1970s, which added detailed procedural restrictions, did not greatly diminish this discretion. Second, these procedural prerequisites to substantial new coal and outer continental shelf oil and gas leasing—such as planning, environmental studies, and public hearings—had already largely been satisfied by the Carter administration.

Third, the basic legislative restriction on how much to lease is embodied in the requirement that coal and outer continental shelf leases be sold for not less than "fair market value." This concept is of course subject to some interpretation. Administrations throughout the 1970s generally assumed the right to reject bids if they fell below the government's estimate of fair value, an approach that some have criticized as interference with the marketplace determination of value.[7] The Reagan administration has moved administratively to reduce this second-guessing, offering more leases no matter how depressed market prices are. This approach, which clearly resembles the policy followed prior to the statutory and administrative reforms of the 1970s, has provoked a lawsuit by environmental groups and ranchers, and continuing criticism from many in Congress.

The fundamental philosophical issue raised—the extent to which the pace of leasing should be determined by private market forces as opposed to governmental judgment about demand and fair prices—has been amply discussed elsewhere.[8] As matters now stand, the Congress has created a

---

5. See, e.g., Hans H. Landsberg and John E. Tilton, "Nonfuel Minerals," in *Current Issues*, pp. 74–116; see also, U.S. Congress, House of Representatives, Subcommittee on Public Lands and National Parks, Committee on Interior and Insular Affairs, *Hearings on Additions to the National Wilderness Preservation System (Mineral Leasing in Wilderness Areas)*, 97th Cong. 2d sess. 1982, (part VII, pp. 253–63), (statement of Daniel Deudney).

6. Although such transfers are only of the right to develop federal minerals, they generally "privatize" the minerals leased because ordinarily the lessee may mine so long as the minerals are produced in paying quantities.

7. See Nelson, "The Public Lands," pp. 43–48.

8. See, e.g., Robert H. Nelson, "Undue Diligence," *Regulation* (January/February 1983).

blue-ribbon commission to examine the matter, and halted new coal leasing pending receipt and review of the commission's recommendations. The debate over leasing is increasingly assuming the proportions of an institutional struggle between the legislative and executive branches; the House Interior Committee attempted to stop Watt from leasing coal by exercising its emergency withdrawal powers under the Federal Land Policy and Management Act, and the administration countered that this power is unconstitutional under the recent Supreme Court decision striking down legislative vetoes.[9] In this atmosphere, the merits of federal resource disposition policy have been substantially submerged.

A related policy initiative of the Reagan administration was to downplay the role of state-federal coal "teams" created by the Carter administration to make recommendations on the timing and location of federal coal leases. Acting on the perception that these teams were too influential and likely to retard the administration's plan for accelerated leasing, Watt proposed revisions that would have greatly diminished their role and, concomitantly, the role of directly affected states and localities. The proposal quickly ran into a buzz saw of criticism from states, local interests, and environmental groups. The states' concerns, expressed with unanimity through the Western Governors' Regional Policy Office, pointed up the basic conflict between the administration's intent to accelerate coal leasing and its avowed "good neighbor" policy. Perhaps the most telling criticism, and the most surprising to the administration, was the opposition of some members of the coal industry itself. Moderate industry interests did not want to lose the political legitimacy that the regional coal teams lent to the coal leasing process, and they feared that a major restructuring of the leasing process would invite a return of the paralysis that had plagued federal coal leasing before the Carter program.

It is difficult to ascertain whether industry concerns or state objections forced the resolution; in either case, in January 1983 the administration formally capitulated, and adopted only modest changes that, if anything, strengthened the role of the regional coal teams. The episode revealed two things. First, the contradiction between the good neighbor policy and the desire to accelerate the privatization of federal coal was resolved, for the time being at least, by emphasizing the former. This result was undoubtedly influenced by the political calculation that the western states, the bedrock of Reagan support, will sooner or later be sufficiently motivated by their lion's share of federal coal leasing revenues to go along with plans for accelerated leasing anyway.

---

9. *Immigration and Naturalization Service* v. *Chada*, 103 S.Ct. 2764 (1983).

Second, the states' stance marked the first time they had united in opposition to a Reagan administration proposal. The administration had been remarkably successful in dampening state opposition and avoiding the "War on the West" sloganeering that had plagued the Carter administration. The governors' successful opposition here and on the question of privatizing federal lands seems likely to embolden them in future dealings with the administration.

The administration's major initiative in oil and gas development (other than leasing in wilderness areas) is former Secretary Watt's intention to accelerate sharply the rate of leasing on the outer continental shelf. Interior Secretary Andrus had proposed to double the rate of outer continental shelf leasing; Secretary Watt proposed to quintuple it, by offering for lease sale about one billion acres, embracing nearly all the prime offshore acreage. This has excited opposition by coastal states as well as environmental groups. Although Watt did move after initial hostility to accommodate the concerns of coastal states, the good neighbor policy seems to be receiving shorter shrift offshore than onshore, most likely because the two factors encouraging conciliation onshore—the concentration of Republican strength in the Rocky Mountain West and the incentive to the states provided by federal sharing of royalties—are mostly absent offshore. Opponents of accelerated leasing have also sought relief from the courts (which have rejected most but not all challenges) and from Congress, which has been flirting with appropriation act riders to bar further leasing off selected areas of the California, Florida, and Massachusetts coasts.

In numerous other ways the Reagan administration has, mostly through Secretary Watt, proposed to accelerate the privatization of federally controlled energy resources. Expansion of oil and gas leasing in national wildlife refuges was proposed; it provoked a lawsuit. In a rare case of proposing legislative reform, the administration has pushed a bill to reduce restrictions on federal oil shale leasing, but the proposal has not met with much interest on Capitol Hill. Instead, substantial progress has been made on compromise legislation by negotiation among affected state and local governments, industry and environmental groups, with the administration sitting on the sidelines. On the other hand, the administration has put aside its ardor for competition long enough to oppose efforts by some in Congress (and supported by the previous administration), to expand the scope of competitive oil and gas leasing onshore, where some 95 percent of the tracts offered are now leased by noncompetitive lottery.

Overall, accelerating mineral development has been at the top of the administration's natural resource agenda. Privatization and decreasing federal regulation are the principal mechanisms used to achieve this goal, and so far the effort has focused almost entirely on administrative changes. Although Congress has been relatively quiescent, that may not last. Because of the inevitable delay in implementing new policies (a lag lengthened by the detailed procedural reforms of the 1970s), actual increases in leasing to date has resulted primarily from the groundwork laid in the Carter administration. The dramatic increase planned by the Reagan administration is just now getting under way. There is still time for Congress to thwart it, and support appears to be growing for restrictive legislation.

Water Resources

During the 1980 campaign, Reagan had made political capital, especially in the West, out of his predecessor's perceived hostility to federal water subsidies manifested in the "War on the West" sloganeering of the press. The administration's avowed dedication to reducing the federal budget, however, seemed to call for continued close scrutiny of the federal role in funding water projects. Federal budget officials had for decades sought to reduce federal water project subsidies, and their hand had been strengthened by increasing opposition from environmental groups and congressional representatives from regions that were largely excluded from such programs.

The administration's response to this dilemma has been politically adroit if not philosophically coherent. First, it has sought to maintain and sometimes increase the level of federal expenditures on water projects already under construction, especially Bureau of Reclamation projects in the West; but it has not actually abandoned the Carter administration's close review of water projects not yet under construction. Indeed, the Reagan administration has toyed with expanding a Carter administration proposal for cost-sharing (requiring nonfederal entities to pay a portion of the costs of new projects); for example, where Carter proposed a relatively modest 10 percent cost-sharing (and was pilloried in the West and in Congress for it), the Reagan administration has been talking of cost-sharing on the order of 35 percent to 50 percent.

Reaction to the Reagan idea, which has not yet been formally announced, has been surprisingly muted in contrast to the vitriol heaped on his predecessor. Clearly there is a marked difference in style. The "hit list" with which President Carter began his administration forever identified him as a fervent opponent of pork-barrel water projects; President Reagan has avoided personal identification with the issue. The principal official identified with Reagan's water policy, Secretary Watt, took the position that water would be the crisis of the 1990s and more federal water projects were vital. In assuming this role, Watt sought with considerable success to cast the Reagan administration as keeper of the flame—the defender of traditional funding of federal water projects against increasingly hostile forces. The contrast with almost every other area of natural resource policy, where Watt and the administration have sought to characterize themselves as dedicated to change and reform, is remarkable.

The administration's other spokesman on water projects, Assistant Secretary of the Army Gianelli, has been more forthright about the need for change in the federal role—probably because the Corps of Engineers operates mostly outside the West. Gianelli has addressed more frankly the fiscal and federalist arguments for federal restraint, and has encouraged not only innovations in funding but also serious reconsideration of projects Congress has authorized but not yet funded. Significantly, no one has called this a "hit list," and neither Watt nor the Bureau of Reclamation has broached the subject of deauthorizing unbuilt reclamation projects.

Soon after taking office, the president moved to scrap the "Principles and Standards" that had been adopted in 1962 (and strengthened under President Carter) in an attempt to bring economic efficiency and environmental quality considerations to the fore in deciding what new water projects deserved federal support. Abolishing these restrictions signaled to traditional water project proponents that political, pork-barrel considerations would assume a larger role. Although Reagan's 1981 executive order on regulatory reform laid heavy emphasis on cost-benefit analyses in environmental regulation, his abolition of the "Principles and Standards" was touted as having the opposite effect on new federal water projects. But the discretion restored by the abolition of the "Principles and Standards" was two-edged, for it freed the Office of Management and Budget (OMB) from having to use the sponsoring agencies' own skewed cost-benefit analyses in deciding the worth of proposed projects.

Ultimately, abolition of the "Principles and Standards" may prove relatively insignificant, for it affects only new projects. In this limited context, however, OMB has played a large role in determining administration support. The few new projects endorsed by this administration are for the most part Corps of Engineers projects where the Corps has obtained significant commitments of local cost-sharing, ranging from 35 percent to 100 percent. The Bureau of Reclamation, operating exclusively in the West, has been left out; apparently the Bureau underestimated the seriousness with which OMB would pursue cost-sharing. But new Secretary of the Interior Clark has promised to go eyeball to eyeball with OMB on new western projects, and few are betting on OMB, at least in an election year.

There is no denying the initial success of the administration's strategy. Its endorsement of the concept of cost-sharing while wavering in its actual implementation has kept both supporters and opponents off balance. Meanwhile, cost-sharing is increasingly being characterized, even by the proponents of the traditional approach, as an idea whose time may be here.

It must be added, however, that advocates of the traditional approach have so far delayed full-scale administration implementation of cost-sharing, and Congress has moved to thwart implementation without legislative approval. The administration has also indicated that its new policy, whatever form it takes, should not apply to projects already under construction. This is a huge concession; those projects will require ten to twenty years and $35 billion to complete at current levels of construction funding.[10] The administration has avoided reducing funds for these projects or seeking greater financial commitments from local sources—for these projects, the policy is business as usual. This stance would lock the traditional pork-barrel in place for many years.

With the election year close at hand, it remains to be seen whether the administration will vigorously press cost-sharing even for new projects. Pork-barrel water projects have, after all, outlasted challenges posed by nearly every administration since Truman's. There is an opportunity now to achieve real reform, but there is considerable doubt that this opportunity will be seized. The tension between the political need to keep the West securely in the administration's corner and the budgetary emphasis on economic efficiency is chronic.[11] It surfaced, for example, in connection with legislation introduced to expand the federal dam safety program. The issue centered on cost-sharing: whether Congress should mandate that local interests bear a substantial percentage of the cost of repairing unsafe dams. The administration has generally tread very lightly here. Although for a time it supported a 30 percent local cost-sharing requirement, it has since retreated and called for a substantial increase in federal funds to be repaid almost totally by the national taxpayer rather than the local beneficiaries. Similarly, the administration early on took a walk on legislation to relax acreage limitations for Western farm operators receiving federally subsidized water. In fact, though Congress conditioned the relaxation on a modest increase in local contributions to the cost of such

---

10. See, e.g., General Accounting Office, *Water Project Construction Backlog—A Serious Problem with No Easy Solution* (RCED-83-49, January 1983).

11. This tension was highlighted, perhaps unwittingly, in the Heritage Foundation transition report that generated many of the Reagan administration's natural resource initiatives. See note 3. That report, strongly free-market in recommending federal land and mineral management reforms, is almost totally devoid of recommendations for water policy reform. It rather lamely observed that "it would not seem wise to attempt a major restructuring of the long tradition of Western agriculture," and that decisions on water projects are ones "which Congress has made wisely in the past and which Congress will continue to do [sic] in the future."

projects, in one of his first acts Secretary Clark proposed legislation to repeal this condition and eliminate the quid pro quo.

As a practical matter, it is likely that federal water project dollars, in the West as in the East, will increasingly be in demand for repair, maintenance, and mitigation of the negative effects of projects already built. The dam safety fight is one example of this; another is provided by the continuing search for federally funded solutions to the increasing salinity of the Colorado River, caused in part by federally subsidized water projects. The need to repair and maintain existing federal projects raises the question of whether such work is a permanent federal obligation. One might expect an administration dedicated to reducing the federal role and controlling domestic expenditures to encourage the private sector to take over such projects or to transfer responsibility for them to state and local governments. Republican Senator Murkowski from Alaska, new to office and plainly unschooled in the folkways of western water politics, suggested just that in 1982; the reaction from the White House has been silence tinged with incredulity. As the administration's latest stands on dam safety funding and acreage limitations show, its policy remains rooted in the status quo. The administration seems bent on committing the federal treasury to permanent responsibility for the western water industry, hardly a position that an aggressively budget-minded administration might be expected to pursue.

In some other areas of traditional federal water project funding—such as flood control, dredging ports, and constructing locks and dams for inland waterways—the administration has followed Carter's lead and been more aggressive in promoting user fees, local cost-sharing, and reduced federal responsibility. The explanation seems obvious: these projects are found almost entirely outside the Republican-dominated West. And even they are scarcely immune to traditional political considerations. For example, the administration has consistently pushed funding for the Tennessee-Tombigbee Waterway, the most expensive water project now under construction, because project proponents such as Senator Stennis play key roles in the defense buildup proposed by the administration.

In sum, the Reagan administration has been inconsistent. It is not much of an exaggeration to describe the administration as waging a two-front war, attacking traditional federal water project funding formulas outside the West, and defending those formulas in the West. The water from projects already built and those under construction is enough to satisfy all but the lowest-priority western needs for many decades. If the federal government assumes a permanent obligation to maintain as well as build dams, the western water industry will have won the fight about which it cares most. Traditional pork-barrel water policies thus remain alive and well, particularly in the West. The contrast with this administration's approach in most other areas is striking.

Even with these glaring exceptions, however, the administration has displayed political skill in maintaining some momentum for long-term water policy reform. The idea of promoting efficiency in federal water project expenditures at least remains alive; although this is a modest achievement, it is so far a real one.

Federal and Indian Water Rights. This topic provoked nearly as much controversy in the 1970s as federal water projects did and for many of the same reasons. The problem is a classic one under federalism: to what extent the federal government will override state law to secure the water necessary to carry out the purposes for which federal and Indian lands are managed and developed. There is no doubt about Congress' power to override state law; instead, the debate has revolved around three main issues: whether Congress has authorized such an override, how much water has been reserved for federal and Indian uses, and how these matters shall be resolved (and if in the courtroom, whether in federal or state court).

Because the problem is concentrated in the West, the interests opposing federal water rights claims tend to be important constituencies of the Reagan administration. Moreover, few federal and Indian claims have been finally settled, and most water supplies have (often with federal assistance) been developed under state law for use by nonfederal interests. Therefore, it was predictable that the Reagan administration would heed the call for a less vigorous assertion of federal water rights.

Yet the magnitude of that retreat is far from clear. The administration has rejected (in a 1982 Department of Justice legal opinion), a controversial Carter administration position on federal water rights claims, but like many other features of this administration's water policy, this position too shows inconsistency. In most essential respects the opinion confirms the expansive interpretations of federal water rights offered by previous administrations, and in at least one respect (federal water rights for acquired federal lands), it lays the basis for even more expansive federal claims. Critical reaction in the West has nevertheless been almost nonexistent; laying a strong legal foundation for asserting federal water rights does not mean they will actually be asserted, and western water users are now confident of the friendship of those who make the decisions. So far, the Reagan administration here has skillfully navigated the gulf that often separates politics from substance, appearance from reality.

The Attorney General did not address the question of Indian water rights. In this area the administration has moved quite cautiously and appears to have made some progress. After twenty years of bruising and mostly inconclusive battles, Indians and non-Indians appear, in some cases at least, to be moving toward each other. The Reagan administration has followed President Carter's lead in openly encouraging such negotiations and has not significantly altered federal positions in the many pending court cases involving Indian water rights. Politically, however, the administration's concerns have been partially, if fortuitously, allayed by several recent Supreme Court decisions that have laid a foundation for cutting back on, and expediting settlement of, Indian claims.

President Reagan vetoed legislation containing one such settlement (involving the Papago tribe in Arizona) on the grounds that the federal government bore too much, and local non-Indians not enough, of the cost of satisfying Indian claims; but the administration did support a later version. By lending its credibility to Indian water rights claims, this administration can make the necessity of settling them more palatable to other western water users. It seems likely that the administration will continue its moderate course, promoting settlements and placing greater emphasis on local responsibility for bearing the costs. This attitude underscores the fact that enhancing the state and local role means more state and local fiscal responsibility as well.

Timber

There are few major timber policy initiatives to evaluate; the timber industry has been in disarray because of the recession-induced decline in building construction. The amount of federal timber sold each year during the Reagan administration has been close to the levels of previous years, and the slack demand has temporarily silenced the calls for increasing it. Moreover, the amount of federal timber actually cut has been substantially less than the amount sold, the backlog of sold but uncut timber has risen to about 40 billion board feet, and the timber industry has sought relief from these sale contracts. Although the issue is being thrashed out largely in Congress, the administration—apparently driven by OMB reluctance to give up timber revenue—opposed bailout legislation in 1982. This opposition has since softened, but a coherent alternative has not yet emerged.

The administration did spark some controversy by moving promptly to rewrite the planning regulations under the National Forest Management Act of 1976, which had undergone extensive scientific and public review before they were adopted in September 1979. President Reagan's Task Force on Regulatory Relief targeted them for revision in March 1981, but the draft revisions published in February 1982 were widely criticized as doing much more than merely streamlining planning; critics alleged that they tilted forest management away from multiple use toward a distinct emphasis on timber production. After substantial further review, most of the provisions of the existing regulations were maintained. Overall, the episode seemed to cost the administration more in credibility than it gained in regulatory relief.

Some revisions did survive, however, including one, long sought by the timber industry, designed to increase the allowable harvest on national forests, by promoting departures from a strict policy of nondeclining even flow (NDEF). The question is, simply stated, whether more timber should in the short term be harvested from the national forests than grows back. Some have argued that departures from this strict sustained-yield principle are often appropriate, especially in replacing relatively stagnant old-growth stands with younger, more vigorous trees.[12] The Forest Service has resisted changing its strict application of the NDEF policy; however, Congress established a carefully defined procedure for such change in the 1976 National Forest Management Act and in 1979 President Carter directed the Forest Service to explore opportunities for doing so.

The current administration has approached the matter more assertively. The applicable planning regulations have been modified to prod local Forest Service managers to include departures from the sustained-yield principle in timber management plans. So far, the effort to facilitate departures from NDEF has been confined to such administrative changes. Because of slack demand and the delay resulting from Congress' requirement that departures from NDEF be incorporated into forest management plans before they can be implemented, there has been no opportunity to observe actual decision making on the question, or to test the results in practice. Controversy seems certain, however, as forest management plans are revised and the industry regains its footing in the economic recovery.

The administration's seemingly fervent embrace of efficiency as a rationale for departing from NDEF has not been applied to another criticized practice of national forest timber harvesting—the selling of timber in marginally productive areas at below-cost prices.[13] Such subsidy of timber sales in marginal areas seems likely to re-emerge as a controversial issue, particularly in relation to wilderness protection, once the economy recovers.

Fish and Wildlife

Most of the administration's policy initiatives with respect to fish and wildlife have been aimed at reducing appropriations for various programs;

---

12. See, e.g., Thomas Lenard, "Wasting Our National Forests," *Regulation* (July/August 1981); Nelson, "The Public Lands," pp. 48–51.

13. Nelson, "The Public Lands," pp. 38–41.

the administration has actively pursued few substantive reforms. President Reagan did respond to the arguments of the western livestock industry by rescinding President Nixon's executive order banning the use of compound 1080 (a poison toxic to a wide variety of wildlife) for predator control on federal rangelands. But this was a limited victory for the ranchers; the final decision rests with the Environmental Protection Agency, where the matter still pends.

In a similar bow to traditional interests, Secretary Watt ended a three-year effort to promulgate regulations implementing the Fish and Wildlife Coordination Act. Passed in 1946, this act was designed to elevate consideration of fish and wildlife values in federal water project design, construction, and operation; but even the law's opponents conceded that it was largely ineffective, partly because there were no implementing regulations. President Carter ordered the Fish and Wildlife Service to prepare regulations, but the process was not completed before Carter left office. Heeding the requests of water project interests and agencies, Secretary Watt simply killed the proposal.

On the other hand, in March 1983 Watt unveiled a rare legislative proposal to increase federal wetlands acquisition (to be underwritten by doubling the price of federal duck hunting stamps and imposing an entry fee at national wildlife refuges). The measure would also prohibit federal agencies from subsidizing projects that would eliminate wetlands, except for federal agricultural price support programs, military activities, "essential" highways and some water projects—exceptions that threatened to swallow the rule. Furthermore, the program would protect only a small fraction of existing wetlands; for the remainder, regulation (and elimination of all federal subsidies for development) is the only reasonable alternative to a massive federal acquisition program. The proposal also conflicts with an Army Corps of Engineers initiative to streamline and reduce the scope of the Clean Water Act's Section 404 permit program, the major federal regulatory means of controlling wetlands destruction. Perhaps for these reasons, the administration's proposal has met with a tepid response on Capitol Hill.

In the highly visible area of endangered species, the administration's policy initiatives can only be described as schizophrenic. The Endangered Species Act had proved by 1980 to be controversial yet popular, and Congress repeatedly resisted efforts to weaken it; but the act's somewhat cumbersome regulatory process threatened traditional activities such as mineral development and water projects, and it seemed ripe for administration attack. The administration first moved to limit the act by essentially halting the listing of new species. The method employed was, ironically, to impose new regulatory burdens (such as a cost-benefit analysis) on the process. The act was due for reauthorization by Congress in 1982, presenting the administration with the opportunity to cement its reforms into law, but the administration shied away from involvement in the legislative process and did not even protest amendments designed to eliminate its own reforms. A modestly revised and strengthened Endangered Species Act consequently moved swiftly through Congress and was signed by the president without fanfare. The listing of endangered species has been resumed.

At about the same time, Secretary Watt undertook to increase attention paid to "recovery" programs, which are designed to enlarge the populations of listed species. These programs were not emphasized by previous administrations, which had instead devoted most of their attention to listing species and designating critical habitats. Given the administration's initial hostility to the Act, Secretary Watt moved with surprising vigor to promote recovery plans.

In sum, the Reagan administration has mounted relatively few initiatives in the fish and wildlife area. Recognizing the popularity of current federal policies and programs, it has acted mainly to reduce federal funding for some wildlife-related activities and to find ways to increase user fees. Its emphasis on deregulation and its responsiveness to traditional commodity interests have prompted some change in regulatory policies, but overall it has so far attempted, and achieved, only modest alterations in these policies.

Grazing Management

Acre for acre, livestock grazing has been the most dominant single use of the federal lands for a century. Although the livestock interests now using the federal rangelands generally have no vested legal rights in their federal grazing permits, as a practical matter the current arrangement gives them substantial control over these lands. Grazing permits have value on the private market, and in many ways the graziers have protected themselves from heavy federal regulation.

In the 1970s the graziers fought a largely defensive battle to maintain their holdings, mostly against challenge by environmentalists. They took the offensive toward the end of the decade, becoming the leading constituency of the sagebrush rebellion. As the Reagan administration took office, a review of federal grazing allotments under new statutes that required multiple-use planning and environmental impact assessment was substantially under way.

The administration has moved without fanfare to decentralize and streamline this review, easing its effects on graziers. It has also taken several other measures to promote grazing, reduce the federal presence, and solidify the hold of livestock interests on the federal range. These changes have all been implemented by administrative directive and regulatory change. The administration has also altered prior policy by allowing livestock operators a free hand to perfect water rights under state law for use on federal multiple use lands, and by refusing to claim federal water rights for significant nongrazing uses on federal multiple use lands.

Finally, and no doubt to its considerable relief, the administration has found a convenient escape from the chronic problem of determining appropriate grazing fees on federal lands. In 1978 Congress established a new interim fee formula that was relatively generous to federal permit holders, and required yet another study of the matter, to be completed by 1985. Although the grazing fee under the interim formula has fallen each year from levels already widely criticized as paltry and inefficient, the administration has so far successfully deflected OMB and House attempts to develop a new formula.

Land Use Planning and Regulation

Consistent with its overall emphasis on revitalizing federalism and reducing domestic federal spending and regulation, the administration has done little to plan or regulate land use. Preservation of prime agricultural farmland was intensively studied during the Carter administration, but nothing of importance was proposed or implemented before Carter left office. Although Secretary of Agriculture Block is said to have supported an executive order providing some federal control on the conversion of farmland to non-agricultural uses, the administration has shown no enthusiasm for this or any other federal presence in the land use area.

The administration did support a congressional cutoff of federally funded flood insurance for developments on barrier islands in certain Atlantic and Gulf of Mexico coastal areas. The idea behind the Coastal Barrier Resources Act of 1982, where environmental and budget-paring interests dovetailed, has reappeared in some other federally subsidized areas, such as wetlands conversion. So far, however, it has not been extended to areas with powerful opposing constituencies, such as water projects, park admission fees, and timber sales in marginally productive areas.

Privatization

Although President Reagan reached out in his campaign to embrace the efforts of western states to gain title to most federal lands within their borders, in its first year his administration did little to advance the avowed objectives of the sagebrush rebellion. Indeed, Secretary Watt quickly redefined the goal of the rebels as seeking not ownership but merely a greater voice in how these lands are managed. (Significantly, Watt never sought to justify his vigorous pursuit of privatization of federal minerals as a response to the sagebrush rebellion; instead, he rested it primarily on national energy security grounds.) A few months afterward, pointing to various steps the administration was taking to give state and local interests more say in federal decisions, Watt proclaimed the rebellion to be both successful and finished, and by late 1981, it appeared that this strategy was working. The sagebrush rebellion and concomitant proposals to dispose of large tracts of federal land were fading rapidly from public view. Significantly, they had never engaged serious attention in Congress.

In early 1982, however, the president himself forcefully revived the question. He issued an executive order creating a federal Property Review Board and announced that several billion dollars would be raised for the federal treasury by selling millions of acres of federal lands through a new Asset Management Program. Though the proposal was limited (parks, wildlife refuges, wilderness areas, and other protectively managed lands were all placed off-limits), it was clearly more than a sale of small, isolated, difficult-to-manage tracts such as the government had been occasionally disposing of for decades. As such, it has involved the administration in a political issue of the first magnitude, with consequences it apparently did not anticipate.

It is tempting to view this proposed land sale as merely an elaboration and further redefinition of the sagebrush rebellion, but such is clearly not the case. For one thing, the official goal of the sagebrush rebellion was to return the federal lands to the states, not to transfer control to private interests. Further, the transaction envisioned by sagebrush rebels was to be free, based on the states' allegedly paramount title to these lands. The states that officially joined the rebellion also were generally careful to emphasize that they wanted these lands to remain in public ownership. In short, selling federal lands to private interests raised a quite different set of policy and political issues.

The land sale proposal actually sprang from the confluence of two forces: an increasingly desperate effort to find new sources of federal revenue,[14] and the arguments of some White House economists that public ownership and management was too inefficient and costly to the government, the economy, and the environment.[15]

---

14. The principal rationale offered by the White House was that a government in financial straits should, like a private business in such circumstances, sell off some assets.

15. The White House group had some supporters in academic circles. See, e.g., Richard L. Stroup and John H. Baden, *Natural Resources: Bureaucratic Myths and Environmental Management* (Cambridge, Mass.: Ballinger Publishing Co., 1983).

It is worth comparing this initiative with the administration's stance on western water project funding. Both land management and water project construction require substantial federal financial commitments that displace and distort the operation of private markets. The administration's politicians clearly have carried the day on federal water projects;[16] in sharp contrast, the economists and budget-cutters succeeded, for at least a time, in significantly influencing administration policy making on privatization.

Part of the explanation for this disparity was the legacy left by the Carter administration's "hit list" of water projects, which brought a much higher level of political concern to water projects, and also gave the Reagan administration an issue to exploit during the campaign. With respect to federal lands, the administration inherited a legacy that seemed to support privatization, but this was true only if it were true that the discontentment with federal management underlying the sagebrush rebellion could be reduced by selling the lands into the private sector. Secretary Watt appreciated the important political distinctions between these courses; he moved promptly to inter the rebellion, and he justified the privatization of federal minerals on somewhat different grounds. But the White House policy makers apparently thought that the rebellion commanded enough political support to make an attempt to implement these conservative Republican principles worthwhile.

Reaction to the privatization proposal suggests that this was a serious miscalculation. With few exceptions, congressional response has ranged from lack of enthusiasm to strenuous opposition. This should not have been a surprise; Congress affirmed as recently as 1976 that federal lands should generally be retained in federal ownership. Furthermore, the bills to transfer federal lands to states that were introduced in the 96th and 97th Congresses attracted little support, even from conservative western Republicans.

The Asset Management Program was not favored by state and local governments because its unveiling largely ended the free transfer of federal lands for recreational purposes. Nearly every western governor has since announced opposition to any significant sales of federal land. Reaction from environmentalists was predictably hostile. More noteworthy was the generally tepid response from the traditional commodity users of federal lands. Although a few warmly embraced the proposals, others opposed it, and most adopted a cautious, wait-and-see attitude.

---

16. Interestingly, then-White House economist Steven Hanke, who helped design the Asset Management Program, advocated privatization of urban water supply systems in an op-ed piece in the *Wall Street Journal* ("Crisis-Ridden Water Systems Should Go Private," September 3, 1981). The administration has, however, rejected all notions of even studying privatization of federal water projects.

Caution seemed prudent; practically every facet of the Asset Management Program was clouded with uncertainty. Although the administration's proposal was to sell only some thirty-five million acres, they were to be chosen from several hundred million acres of federal land, and procedures and guidelines for identifying the particular lands to be sold were left ambiguous. Moreover, it was not clear whether existing users were to be protected, whether they or state and local governments would be given a preferential right of purchase, whether sales would be by public auction, how mineral interests would be disposed of, how the sales would be timed, the extent to which they would be geographically dispersed, and so forth. These uncertainties made interested parties more anxious and made it difficult for the administration to generate strong support for the program.

Resolving these ambiguities would require the administration to resolve a tension between its politics and its philosophy. The political process does not fully share economists' preoccupation with efficiency;[17] although ranchers were a primary constituency behind the sagebrush rebellion, they quickly perceived that they would lose out to energy companies, recreational developers, and others if the federal lands they now control were put up for competitive bidding. But if the marketplace is the most efficient way of deciding how land is to be used, competitive bidding would seem essential.[18] The difficulty of reconciling these competing impulses has further slowed the Asset Management Program.

The administration has also been indecisive about the role of Congress. The administration conceded that statutory authority for significant sales of national forest lands is lacking, and promised in early 1982 to propose legislation to secure this authority and to establish sale terms and procedures, but it has not yet done so. With respect to lands managed by the Bureau of Land Management (BLM), the administration has promised to cooperate with Congress, but it has not abandoned the argument that it already has legal authority to sell BLM lands despite the retention philosophy reflected in the Federal Land Policy and Management Act. Lawsuits have already been filed to challenge the program.

In the face of this lukewarm response, the administration has appeared to be discomfited and in some disarray. It has retreated on the goals of the program, now emphasizing that at most only a "few million" acres will be

---

17. See, e.g., George Stigler, "Economists and Public Policy," *Regulation* (May/June 1982).

18. Some have argued that high federal management costs and low productivity make even an outright gift of federal grazing lands to ranchers financially beneficial to the federal treasury. See Robert H. Nelson, "A Long Term Strategy for the Public Lands," in *Resource Conflicts in the West* (Reno, Nev.: Nevada Public Affairs Institute, U. of Nevada, 1983), p. 119.

sold. It no longer characterizes the program as a true test of conservative Republican principles, but instead pictures the effort as a modest, uncontroversial attempt to rid the federal landholdings of isolated, difficult-to-manage parcels serving no important national interest. Secretary Watt's second annual report quietly noted that in response to the president's call for "better" management of federal assets, 2.7 million acres of Bureau of Land Management land, none in areas of "national environmental significance," had been "identified."[19] The secretary saw no reason to inform his readers explicitly why this land had been "identified"; i.e., for disposal.[20]

Ironically, the disposal of isolated, difficult-to-manage parcels of federal land might have been carried out without controversy. But the administration's political miscalculation—that the sagebrush rebellion meant support for privatization—has destroyed its ability to accomplish that objective in much the same way that the Carter administration's water project "hit list" greatly hampered its efforts to reform federal water policy. The privatization program contains the seeds of a renewed "War on the West," and furthermore dramatizes the tension that has always existed between conservative Republican principles and the political and financial benefits flowing from the large federal landholdings in the Republican-dominated West.

Wilderness

Wilderness designation and management have involved the Reagan administration in more controversy than perhaps any other question. The issue offers the classically simple choice between development and preservation; however, a little background is necessary to understand the Reagan initiatives.[21]

Some federal lands were affirmatively managed in a way that would preserve their natural character as early as the 1920s, but it was not until the 1960s that Congress generally confirmed this practice and supplied a statutory base for such protective management. The Wilderness Act of 1964 established the National Wilderness Preservation System (NWPS), designated the charter areas of the system (some nine million acres of national forest land), and

---

19. See note 2.

20. Secretary Watt's retreat has been sharply criticized by one of the architects of the Asset Management Program. Steven H. Hanke, "Watt Never Did Believe in Privatizing U.S. Lands," *Wall Street Journal* (August 5, 1983), p. 18.

21. The discussion here has little applicability to Alaska, where wilderness issues were largely resolved by the 1980 Alaska National Interest Lands Conservation Act.

established a framework for managing designated areas and designating new ones.

Congress struck several management compromises in 1964. For example, mineral activity was allowed to continue in designated national forest wilderness under some restrictions, but no new mining rights could be created after December 31, 1983. Looking also to consider new areas for designation as wilderness, Congress mandated review of all undeveloped areas in the national parks and wildlife refuges, but only some 10 percent of undeveloped areas in the national forests. Although it did not forbid agency management of undesignated lands for preservation, Congress reserved for itself the right to decide whether to include new areas within the NWPS.

The national forests have been the scene of most wilderness battles; the objective of multiple use which prevails there makes conflict with wilderness preservation certain, and about a third of these forests, or sixty million acres, are roadless and thus potentially qualify for wilderness protection. (Parks and wildlife refuges contain many fewer qualifying acres and are already off limits to most wilderness-impairing uses.) Although Congress did not formally require a comprehensive wilderness review of the national forests, the Forest Service embarked in the early 1970s on a program to identify and make recommendations for all its potential wilderness areas. This review process, the first Roadless Area Review and Evaluation (RARE I), was completed in the mid-1970s amid controversy and litigation. The Carter administration undertook a new review, RARE II, which was completed in 1979. RARE II resulted in recommendations to Congress that about 15 million acres be added forthwith to the NWPS, 11 million acres be subject to further study, and 36 million acres be given over to ordinary multiple use management. This review, too, was plagued by controversy and court challenges.

In 1976 Congress mandated a wilderness review for all BLM-managed public lands, about 24 million acres of which BLM had, by 1980, identified as having wilderness characteristics. Further, although Congress had added park, refuge, and national forest areas to the NWPS, legislative designation was proceeding relatively slowly. When the Reagan administration assumed office some 75 million acreas of federal multiple use lands in the lower forty-eight states were subject to congressional consideration for protection as wilderness.

The wilderness issues facing the new administration could be divided into three categories: management of existing NWPS areas, and particularly the extent to which new mineral activities would be allowed as closure of the twenty-year "window" on new mineral development drew near; management of undesignated areas up for congressional consideration (specifically, what kinds of intrusions—timber harvesting, road building, mineral development—

to allow); and administration recommendations to Congress on areas up for legislative designation.

The administration took office evincing considerable skepticism toward wilderness preservation. Its emphasis on natural resource exploitation (particularly minerals), its friendliness to commodity users traditionally hostile to preservation, and its pillorying of "extremist preservationists" combined to mark the wilderness issue as a major battleground. In mid-1981 a directive from Secretary Watt instructing subordinates to find ways to "open wilderness areas" leaked to the press, and the battle was on. The first skirmish involved the Bob Marshall Wilderness Area in Montana, one of the charter areas in the system and named for one of the patron saints of the wilderness movement. When the administration moved to authorize mineral exploration in the area, the House Interior Committee invoked its emergency withdrawal power. Although Watt backed off, the administration supported industry's challenge to the committee's order in federal court. At the same time, the administration took steps to exploit the mineral development "window" in other designated national forest wilderness. Whereas previous Secretaries of the Interior[22] had interpreted the Wilderness Act as allowing, not requiring, the issuance of mineral leases, Watt initially took the position that such leasing was in fact required and would therefore be pursued.

The wide publicity given these initiatives crystallized public opinion and mobilized a substantial effort throughout the country, including the West, to protect wilderness. The environmental extremists derided by Watt soon found that their sympathizers on this issue included Republican congressional stalwarts in most of the western states, and the administration was quickly put on the defensive. Pressure mounted in Congress, and after the House Interior Committee recommended a six-month moratorium on mineral leasing in wilderness areas in November 1981, the administration backtracked. It embraced and extended this moratorium through the 1982 election, and then sought to salvage some ground by proposing its own Wilderness Protection Act of 1982.

Although it was touted as a protection for wilderness areas, the administration's proposed act was riddled with loopholes and exceptions. It would actually have weakened existing protections by, for example, automatically opening wilderness areas to mineral development in the year 2000 unless Congress provided otherwise, and giving the president immediate authority to open wilderness areas to development on national security grounds. This proposal fueled congressional opposition to wilderness exploration, and in August 1982 the House overwhelmingly passed a bill to ban new leasing in

---

22. The Department of the Interior oversees mineral leasing on all federal lands, including the national forests, although the Forest Service is housed in the Department of Agriculture.

all designated and most potential wilderness areas. Fifty-four Senators co-sponsored identical legislation in the Senate, but Senator McClure, chairman of the key committee, refused to move it. In the session's closing hours a rider was added to an appropriation act to extend the moratorium on leasing to October 1, 1983. Secretary Watt backed off even further, announcing that he would issue no new leases in any designated wilderness through 1983. The extent of this retreat was underscored by Watt's decision to apply the same no-leasing policy to areas under congressional consideration for designation.[23]

That announcement ended the immediate controversy over mineral leasing, but it did not take the wilderness issue off the legislative or executive agenda. The next phase began in the fall of 1982, when a federal court of appeals ruled that the Forest Service's RARE II environmental impact statement (EIS) was inadequate to support immediate development of some 40 million acres of potential wilderness that the agency had recommended not be designated as wilderness. The court specifically found the EIS adequate for the 15 million acres that the Forest Service had recommended be designated as wilderness, but the administration chose to ignore that distinction and in January 1983 began a third RARE review of all the lands on which Congress had not yet acted. This directive was accompanied by one that accelerated efforts to clear away all procedural obstacles to wilderness-impairing developments. At the same time, Watt announced that more than a million acres of potential wilderness would be dropped from further study on technical grounds. Thus the administration once again challenged Congress and wilderness advocates.

Similarly, the administration generally opposed wilderness designation proposals pending in Congress. Even before RARE III was announced, the administration had disavowed a number of the Carter administration's recommendations, testified in opposition to several pending designation proposals, and called on Congress to "release" all areas not designated for immediate, permanent, non-wilderness management. The 97th Congress nevertheless passed a few wilderness designation bills, only one of which the president vetoed. Sensitive to the fact that he was the first president ever to veto a wilderness bill, President Reagan chose to justify his veto on fiscal grounds.

Congress still must act on numerous wilderness designation proposals, and current administration policy could subject many national forest roadless

---

23. Although Congress had in the late 1970s forbidden the Secretary of the Interior to engage in mineral leasing in some specific wilderness study areas, many had legally remained open to mineral leasing at the Secretary's discretion. Secretary Watt in effect chose not to exercise this authority in the face of congressional and public reaction.

areas to wilderness-impairing activities relatively soon. Furthermore, although BLM wilderness study areas are for the most part protected by law until Congress acts, the administration may try to relax or eliminate these protections by administrative interpretation. It may also become the first one to propose to redesignate some statutorily protected wilderness areas for other uses. Although the administration is in retreat, then, it is not yet routed, and the wilderness issue is far from dead.

The Reagan administration's record on wilderness brings the Carter administration's water project "hit list" to mind. In both cases the administration's stance generated wide publicity, supplying material for political cartoonists and provoking editorial reactions all over the country. In both cases the administration's position was perceived as intransigent, and quickly came to be rather widely regarded as extreme. In both cases the administration's position on a single issue became emblematic of its natural resource policy in the eyes of the general public, with sometimes damaging results to its other policy initiatives. Public reaction in both cases forced congressional members of the president's party to run for cover, isolating and placing the administration on the defensive. Both the water project and wilderness battles eventually became institutional struggles, with Congress asserting its prerogatives against threatened incursions by the executive. The policy merits of both issues paled almost to the point of irrelevancy.

Although the similarities are striking, considerable irony can be found in the differences between the executive and legislative branches on these two issues. The Carter episode saw an administration sensitive to environmental quality and pork-barrel inefficiencies attack a congressional sacred cow, water resources development projects, which embodied progress as defined by economic materialism and achieved by conquering natural forces. The wilderness fight four years later saw these roles largely reversed, with the administration advancing material goals to be achieved by dominating nature, and Congress defending natural systems and protecting spiritual and aesthetic values.

In one respect, the Reagan administration's miscalculation on the wilderness issue was understandable. The unexpected decline in oil prices resulting from OPEC's disarray undercut a chief reason for exploiting wilderness (to allow oil and gas development), even as that decline benefited the administration in many other ways. But the strength of public support for wilderness is not explained by that fact alone. It remains to be seen whether the wilderness issue will plague this administration as the water project issue plagued the last one. President Carter was perceived as never retreating from his stance on water projects, even though he eventually yielded a good deal. He could gain no credit either way, for compromise or for redirecting federal water policy. The Reagan administration seems to be reaching the same status in its hostility to wilderness. It too may achieve some victories, but the political cost will probably be great, and the compromises that may emerge will probably earn it no political credit from anyone—developers, preservationists, or Congress.

The Reagan administration's intransigence on the wilderness issue has done more to advance wilderness preservation than perhaps any other event or policy. Although the wilderness issue involves less than 15 percent of the federal land base, it hangs like a cloud over nearly all federal natural resource policy, and will continue to do so for at least another five to ten years. Proposals to increase timber harvesting or mineral development, improve rangeland management, build new water projects, and dispose of federal lands are all politically related to wilderness preservation. Wilderness commands an increasing share of the attention Congress can devote to natural resource questions, squeezing out other issues in the process. By galvanizing public sentiment toward wilderness preservation and against its own policy, the administration is undercutting its other natural resource initiatives.

This suggests that it may well be in the administration's overall interest to move promptly to promote generous legislative designations of wilderness. The resources that would be rendered inaccessible are relatively small,[24] and these resources are for the most part inaccessible anyway. These areas are by definition remote and thus costly to develop, and development of potential wilderness has been rare for the past several decades, even where it was legally possible. Ultimately, Congress and the courts both have ways to overcome a determined executive, and wilderness developers cannot or will not tolerate the uncertainty and extra cost that result. In any event, wilderness designation is only statutory; it can be undone by a simple act of legislation. Although removing areas from the NWPS will never be easy, the easier it is to put areas in, the easier it may become to pull them out.

From a broader policy perspective, then, the administration has lost an opportunity to defuse the wilderness issue, to earn credit with wilderness supporters (who are plainly more numerous than the administration had thought), and to clear the decks for other, more important policy initiatives. Wilderness preservation has become a motherhood-and-apple-pie issue in remarkably short order. It is also proving to be a political lightning rod, shaping the public's attitude toward more mundane but economically more significant issues of natural resource policy. In short, the political nerve touched by the

---

24. See, e.g., *Hearings on Additions to the National Wilderness Preservation System*, pp. 253–77.

Reagan administration's handling of the wilderness issue may, barring a major shift in policy, be difficult to soothe.

Conclusion

The Reagan administration's performance in natural resources policy has not matched the relative clarity and ambitiousness of its program goals. Having decided not to seek major changes in natural resources legislation, it has had to rely primarily on administrative reforms. And although the administration has pursued some reforms rather aggressively, in other areas it has readily sacrificed program goals to political advantage. Its willingness to eschew legislative reforms has isolated it from Congress, an isolation exacerbated by the stridency and confrontational style of administration policy makers such as former Secretary Watt.

Much of the administration's promised freshness and boldness in natural resource policy making has been squandered in unpopular initiatives such as the privatization program and the assault on wilderness. The administration's remaining credibility and political capital may be more effectively devoted to other reforms, particularly now that Watt is no longer Secretary of the Interior, but it may be difficult even for a second Reagan administration to make significant headway. Substantial effort will be necessary to repair its credibility in the country at large and to restore close working relations with Congress. Also, many of the areas ripe for meaningful reform, such as water project policy, pit the administration against vocal interests in Republican strongholds. So far the administration has rarely allowed philosophical objectives to override partisan political advantage, and it has largely refrained from the consensus-building necessary to fashion meaningful, lasting reform.

In this process some moderate business interests have become disaffected. Those doing business within the framework of federal natural resource policy prefer that an administration provide a reasonable degree of stability and avoid creating a political atmosphere in which private natural resource companies are seen as callous exploiters unconcerned with the nation's well-being. The Reagan administration has provided neither. Its rhetoric of change and pursuit of administrative reforms without congressional sanction has undercut the base of certainty provided by the compromises and reforms of the previous dozen years. Its stridency and seeming overeagerness to serve business interests has undercut business credibility with an American public increasingly concerned with environmental quality and preservation. That the rhetoric of the natural resources debates of the 1980s largely echoes the polarization that often marked the previous years is thus viewed by moderate business interests as objectionable rather than laudable. The administration's policies and style have alienated many of those whose interests it is purportedly advancing.

Underneath its ambitious rhetoric, then, the Reagan administration's performance in natural resource policy has produced few dramatic departures or lasting changes. By preaching the need for a fundamentally different course, the Reagan administration has asked to be judged by that standard, and by that measure, it has failed.

ENVIRONMENTAL POLICY

Robert W. Crandall and Paul R. Portney

Even while the Reagan administration and many of its policies were holding up well in public opinion polls, its record on environmental protection was a source of concern to many within the administration and a cause of outrage to many outside it. Alleged malfeasance and incompetence at the Environmental Protection Agency (EPA) led in the spring of 1983 to the resignation or dismissal of the administrator, the deputy administrator, and virtually every other top agency official. This upheaval has obscured overall analysis of the EPA in the Reagan administration, an analysis central to understanding the administration's environmental policies.

The furor over environmental regulatory policy has led some to conclude that all would be well if the nation returned to pre-1981 policies. This view is seriously in error; this country's efforts at environmental protection were encountering very serious problems well before President Reagan's initial appointees to EPA began adding to them. However, although these inherited difficulties presented certain problems to the fledgling administration, they also represented an opportunity to reshape environmental protection in a simpler, more effective, and less expensive form—an opportunity that has largely been lost.

Environmental Regulation Through 1980

By 1980, the problems of environmental regulation were of several sorts. They included very long delays on the part of the EPA in issuing ambient and individual source discharge standards, widespread noncompliance with

47

many of the standards that had been issued, a monitoring system that made it difficult to know which areas or sources were in violation of EPA standards and which were not, an enforcement program that made it highly unlikely that areas or sources found to be in violation would have an incentive to comply quickly, and a very questionable scientific basis for many of the most important standards.

Standard Setting

Consider first the delays in establishing ambient and effluent standards. Under the 1977 amendments to the Clean Air Act, the EPA was directed to review by the end of 1980 all of the National Ambient Air Quality Standards (NAAQSs) it had issued in the early 1970s, and to propose new standards as required. In spite of the importance of these standards (in effect, they provide the goals for the country's overall air quality management program), the EPA managed to revise only one of the six NAAQSs by the deadline. The Reagan administration also inherited a backlog of 643 proposed changes in State Implementation Plans (SIPs) that were awaiting approval by the EPA. The SIPs detail the states' plans for controlling existing polluters to bring air quality in each state into conformance with the national standards. The delay in approving these proposed plans was both hampering state control efforts and creating uncertainty for those being regulated.

Nor were these the only problems in air quality management. Amendments to the Clean Air Act passed in 1970 had gone beyond the regulation of common (or "criteria") air pollutants. They also directed the EPA to publish a list of, and develop regulations for, sources of other "hazardous" air pollutants that could pose a threat to health. Ten years later, in spite of a review by the EPA itself that identified forty-three potentially hazardous substances, the agency had listed only seven substances as hazardous and had established discharge standards for sources of just four of these substances.[1]

An additional major responsibility of the EPA under the Clean Air Act is the establishment of New Source Performance Standards—limits on discharges of the criteria air pollutants that apply to all new or substantially modified sources. Despite their obvious importance, by 1980 EPA had yet to establish such standards for a number of important types of facilities, including industrial boilers—which account for 10 percent of annual emissions of sulfur dioxide in the United States.

---

1. The Conservation Foundation, *State of the Environment 1982* (Washington, D.C.: 1983), p. 64.

Conditions were not much better in other areas at the EPA. For example, the 1972 amendments to the Federal Water Pollution Control Act (now called the Clean Water Act) directed the EPA administrator to establish discharge standards for individual sources of conventional or common water pollutants. By 1980, seven years after the date specified, there were no effluent standards for a number of major industries, including such substantial dischargers as the organic chemicals and metal finishing industries.

Comparable delays existed under other EPA regulatory programs. For example, by the end of 1980 no testing rules had been promulgated under Section 4 of the Toxic Substances Control Act (TSCA), although there are probably more than 50,000 chemicals currently in commerce and many are believed to pose serious threats to health. Nor was there much activity under the other substantive sections of the act. The slow pace of activity under TSCA was a source of great frustration to environmentalists and, arguably, the business community as well.

A similar picture could be painted for regulation under the Resource Conservation and Recovery Act of 1976 (RCRA), the federal statute empowering the EPA to regulate the generation, handling, transportation, storage, and disposal of hazardous wastes. In May 1980, under court order, the EPA finally issued rules pertaining to several classes of hazardous waste handlers. Although these regulations did provide for the collection of information about hazardous wastes, they glossed over perhaps the most important issue to be addressed under RCRA—the technical requirements that surface impoundments and land disposal sites would have to meet if they were to be used for hazardous wastes. Thus, by the end of 1980 EPA had not addressed the fundamental problem of hazardous wastes.

Enforcement and Monitoring

The state of compliance with EPA standards also left much to be desired. Consider the status of state efforts to bring air quality into compliance with the NAAQSs. According to the National Commission on Air Quality, by the end of 1980 there were 489 counties in the United States in which the ambient air quality standard for ozone was not being met. The population of these counties was nearly 144 million, more than 60 percent of the population of the United States. In twenty-one large metropolitan areas the ozone standard was being exceeded by at least 50 percent, and in Los Angeles the standard was being exceeded by 325 percent.[2]

---

2. National Commission on Air Quality, *To Breathe Clean Air* (Washington, D.C.: U.S. Government Printing Office, 1981), p. 3.4–6.

Conditions were better with respect to the other criteria air pollutants, although noncompliance with the NAAQSs was far from isolated. In forty-four counties air quality failed to meet the NAAQSs for total suspended particulate matter (thought to be one of the most harmful of the common air pollutants); 40 counties were in violation of the carbon monoxide standard, with parts of 105 other counties also in violation and 18 counties were in violation of the standard for sulfur dioxide.[3]

Nor could one argue that time would take care of these problems. The National Commission on Air Quality predicted that even by 1987, at least seven major metropolitan areas, containing 35 million people, would still be in violation of the ozone standard. The commission also foresaw that violations of several other NAAQSs would persist, although none would be as serious as the ozone standard violations.

Unfortunately, it is difficult to know how much confidence to place in the data on noncompliance with the national air standards, because the nationwide monitoring network on which the EPA relies is seriously deficient. According to the General Accounting Office (GAO), there were about 5,300 air pollution monitors of all sorts reporting to the EPA in early 1981.[4] Although this seems to be a substantial number, it amounts to only one monitor per 670 square miles. Moreover, since most of the monitors are located in or near large metropolitan areas, virtually no monitoring is done in rural areas. This is difficult to explain in view of the many studies that have shown a link between elevated levels of air pollution and reduced agricultural production.

There also appear to be serious problems with many of the air pollution monitors that are in place. The GAO found in 1981 that only 59 percent of the EPA's National Air Monitoring Sites met all the requirements for siting, operation, and certification. Only 45 percent of the State and Local Air Monitoring Sites (for use by states in determining compliance) met these requirements, which were established by the EPA.[5] An earlier GAO random audit of the EPA's air monitoring network produced even more discouraging results. Of the 243 monitors evaluated in that check, 81 percent failed to meet at least one of the criteria for reliable monitoring. Of the 106 ozone, carbon monoxide, and nitrogen dioxide monitors evaluated in that review, all but six failed for one or more reasons.[6] Not all of the deficiencies cited by the GAO

---

3. Ibid., pp. 3.4–29 to 3.4–5.
4. U.S. General Accounting Office, *Problems in Air Monitoring System Affect Data Reliability*, Report CED-82-101 (September 22, 1982), p. i.
5. Ibid., pp. 8–9.
6. U.S. General Accounting Office, *Air Quality: Do We Really Know What It Is?*, Report CED-79-84 (May 31, 1979), p. 5.

are critical, but these figures do give one pause in interpreting data on the attainment status of air quality control regions around the country.

What about the compliance record of the individual sources regulated by the EPA under the major environmental statutes? Here, too, there was reason to be concerned as the Reagan administration prepared to take office. Consider the effluent guidelines established under the Clean Water Act. In addition to the industrial sources that the EPA regulates, municipal waste treatment plants must also get discharge permits from the EPA. In 1979, the GAO randomly audited 242 waste treatment plants in the Boston, Chicago, and San Francisco areas.[7] Of this total, 211 (87 percent) violated the terms of their effluent discharge permits for at least one of the twelve months for which the plants were monitored. Moreover, 56 percent of the plants were in violation for more than half the year.

The GAO also looked into the degree of violation at the 211 offending plants. Nearly a third were in what the GAO called "serious" violation— not only was the plant in violation of at least one of its limits for four consecutive months, but its actual discharge was at least 50 percent above the limit during that period.[8]

Similar, although somewhat less discouraging, problems existed in the source monitoring program under the Clean Air Act. The EPA claims that compliance with air pollution discharge standards runs about 90 percent among major polluters (those emitting more than 100 tons of a pollutant per year).[9] Recent data seem to confirm this figure.[10] However, this is not as reassuring as it appears. In 1979 the GAO investigated the means by which the compliance status of sources was determined. Of 19,973 major sources reported to be in full compliance in 1977, only 498 had been tested by comparing actual stack emissions with permitted levels. In 4,462 cases, the determination that a source was complying was based on an inspection of the facility during which the pollutant concentration of the fuels may have been sampled or the pollution control equipment observed. In 14,458 of the cases (nearly 75 percent), a source was deemed to be in compliance based on a written report sent by the source itself to the relevant state agency.

Recent data indicate increased reliance on better means of determining compliance. For example, of 13,304 major air polluters reported to be in compliance in 1981, source certification (the least reliable method) accounted

7. U.S. General Accounting Office, *Costly Wastewater Treatment Plants Fail to Perform As Expected*, Report CED-81-9 (November 14, 1980).

8. Ibid, p. 11.

9. U.S. General Accounting Office, *Improvements Needed in Controlling Major Air Pollution Sources*, Report CED-78-165 (January 2, 1979), p. 6.

10. Information supplied by the Environmental Protection Agency.

for only 36 percent.[11] Inspections were the basis for 60 percent of the compliance determinations, and stack tests accounted for the remaining 4 percent. Thus, although self-certification is apparently on the wane, stack tests of actual emissions still account for a very small percentage of compliance determinations.

Data from the earlier GAO audit give reason to be cautious even about this apparent improvement. The GAO audited 921 sources reported to be in compliance with their air pollution limits. Two hundred of these, or 22 percent, were not in compliance at all. In one EPA region, 52 percent of the sources supposedly in compliance in fact were not.[12]

What about the sources that were determined to be out of compliance? Was there any incentive for them to comply? In 1978 the GAO undertook a review of emission sources that had been in violation of their standards in earlier years. The study found that 70 percent of the sources that had been subject to some kind of enforcement action since 1973 were still not in compliance by 1977. The GAO also audited one EPA region and found that neither the states nor the EPA had taken any kind of enforcement action against half of the 321 major sources not in compliance at the end of 1977.[13]

The Scientific Basis for Standard Setting

The scientific basis for several of the important NAAQSs in effect in 1980 highlights not only the difficulty of standard setting, but also the public health tradeoffs the nation was forced to make under the major environmental statutes. Under the Clean Air Act, for example, the administrator of the EPA is directed to establish national air quality standards that will provide an "adequate margin of safety" against adverse health effects. This implies that there is some level of pollution below which no adverse health effects occur—a "threshold" concentration. Setting the NAAQSs has, in effect, been a search for this threshold.

However, clinicians and epidemiologists are becoming convinced that there is *no* perfectly safe level for any air pollutant. Some individuals are so sensitive to pollution (because of age, respiratory disease, or other conditions), it appears that virtually any concentration can cause them some harm or discomfort. Thus, under a very strict reading of the Clean Air Act, maximum permissible concentrations of the common air pollutants should be set at zero or at a natural "background" level. Yet this is clearly untenable; it implies

11. Information supplied by the Environmental Protection Agency.
12. U.S. General Accounting Office, *Improvements Needed*, p. 9.
13. Ibid., p. 16.

an end to all fossil fuel combustion, indeed to all current industrial activity—an outcome that Congress clearly did not intend and would not abide.

As a result, standard setting under the Clean Air Act has been an uneasy review of the clinical, animal, and epidemiological studies linking air pollution to health impairments. Economic and other practical considerations are surely taken into account in setting standards, even if no one is willing to admit it. For example, when the EPA proposed a revision of the NAAQSs for carbon monoxide in 1980, it defined the population to be protected as persons with angina pectoris, although some argued that hemolytic anemics would not be protected against health impairment at the proposed standard level.[14]

Despite this definition of the sensitive population, there is evidence that the health protection offered by reduced carbon monoxide had a very high cost indeed. According to the Regulatory Analysis and Review Group of the Executive Office of the President, comparison of the 9 parts per million (ppm) carbon monoxide standard that the EPA was proposing with a less strict alternative, 12 ppm, showed that each sick day prevented by the stricter standard would cost the nation between $6,000 and $250,000.[15] Although the health of those with cardiovascular disease is very important, it is far from obvious that the prevention of one sick day is worth $6,000—much less a quarter of a million dollars.

Nor was this the only case where standard setting was both difficult and economically significant. When the EPA revised the NAAQSs for ozone in 1979, it based its proposed revision on a number of clinical and epidemiological studies that left much to be desired. One of the key studies used only six subjects, two of whom were the researchers conducting the study![16] In another key study, there was no control for sulfates and other potentially important air pollutants, nor was any attempt made to control for the smoking habits of the subjects or for histories of respiratory disease.[17] Several other studies that the EPA considered had serious shortcomings as well.[18] If studies

---

14. Council on Wage and Price Stability, "Environmental Protection Agency National Ambient Air Quality Standards for Carbon Monoxide," Report of the Regulatory Analysis Review Group (November 25, 1980), p. 26.

15. Ibid., p. 65. The report also points out, however, that if other groups besides angina patients benefit from the 9 ppm standard, the cost effectiveness of that standard can improve dramatically. See pp. 66–67.

16. A.J. DeLucia and W.C. Adams, "Effects of Ozone Inhalation During Exercise on Pulmonary Function and Blood Biochemistry," *Journal of Applied Physiology*, vol. 43, no. 1 (1977), pp. 75–81.

17. D.I. Hammer et al., "The Los Angeles Student Nurse Study," *Archives of Environmental Health*, vol. 28 (1974), pp. 255–268.

18. For a discussion of these studies, see Christopher H. Marraro, "Revising the Ozone Standard," in Lester B. Lave, ed., *Quantitative Risk Assessment in Regulation* (Washington, D.C.: Brookings Institution, 1983), pp. 55–98.

such as these constitute the bulk of the evidence for setting standards, it is difficult to see how the administrator of EPA could find a threshold concentration even if one existed.

As in the case of carbon monoxide, the analysis conducted during the revision of the ozone standard raised serious questions about the wisdom of basing air quality standards on health evidence alone. The White House Council on Wage and Price Stability (CWPS) reviewed both the 0.10 ppm ozone standard that the EPA had originally proposed and a less stringent standard of 0.12 ppm. Using estimates of reductions in exposure of individuals sensitive to ozone, and estimates of the added costs of meeting the tighter standard, the CWPS was able to estimate the cost of preventing one person-hour of exposure to the levels of ozone that would have resulted from the less stringent standard.[19] Attributing the full incremental cost of the tighter standard to those individuals designated as the sensitive population, the CWPS found that the 0.10 ppm standard would cost the nation between \$2,000 and \$4,000 for each person-hour of exposure prevented. Again, this suggests that even if a threshold concentration were identifiable, it might occur at such a low level that a slightly higher standard would be preferred in view of the associated savings. However, if the tighter standard resulted in additional health or other types of beneficial effects, the cost per person-hour of unhealthy exposure to ozone would be reduced, perhaps considerably.

Other Considerations

By the end of the 1970s it was clear that environmental protection was expensive. According to the Council on Environmental Quality, the United States was spending more than \$40 billion per year by 1980 to comply with federal government regulations; from 1980 to 1989, the council estimated, an additional \$580 billion would be required. Such sums make it imperative that environmental rules be effective and efficient.

On the subject of effectiveness, the record is mixed although air quality does appear to have improved during the 1970s. Although the monitoring data are not all that they should be, they suggest that concentrations of sulfur dioxide and particulate matter declined by roughly 20 percent and 7 percent, respectively, and carbon monoxide concentrations fell by 40 percent at urban locations. However, ozone concentrations are apparently unchanged, and ambient concentrations of nitrogen dioxide actually increased.

---

19. For an excellent discussion of the report of the Council on Wage and Price Stability and the events surrounding the revision of the ozone standards, see Lawrence J. White, *Reforming Regulation: Processes and Problems* (Englewood Cliffs, N.J.: Prentice-Hall, 1981), pp. 47–70.

Because concentrations of these pollutants are affected not only by control efforts but also by economic fluctuations, changes in fuel prices, monitor locations, population migration, and other factors, it is difficult to attribute all of the changes in air quality to the Clean Air Act. Air quality may have improved more rapidly in the 1960s than in the 1970s, although federal involvement began in earnest in 1970. Nevertheless, air quality controls probably played a role in the improvements realized.

Water quality apparently did not improve during the 1970s. Water quality is more difficult to measure than air quality because the monitoring data are even less reliable. After examining the data that do exist, the Council on Environmental Quality concluded in 1980 that ". . . the quality of surface waters has not changed much in the last five years."[20] (Earlier data are not available even though water pollution legislation dates back to the 1960s). The Conservation Foundation drew the same conclusion more recently, writing that ". . . nationally, there has been little change in water quality over the past seven years—at least with respect to the 'conventional' pollutants."[21] This is despite the expenditure of $22.5 billion on municipal sewage treatment plants between 1972 and 1980 and comparable expenditures for industrial water pollution control. If groundwater is included in this assessment, a much more pessimistic conclusion is possible: recent evidence suggests that there is increasing contamination of underground aquifers, primarily by leachate from hazardous waste disposal sites.

By preventing the deterioration of, for example, air or water quality, regulatory programs can be effective even if there is no improvement in environmental quality. From 1970 to 1980, U.S. industrial production increased by about 36 percent, while the number of automobiles on the road and the number of vehicle miles traveled increased by more than half.[22] The fact that air quality improved in these years, while water quality apparently did not deteriorate, can be adduced in support of the regulations.

Summary

In spite of some positive accomplishments, environmental regulation was troubled when the Reagan administration took office. Among other problems were considerable delays on the part of the EPA in issuing important ambient and source discharge standards; widespread violations of the standards

---

20. *Environmental Quality: 1980*, The Eleventh Annual Report of the Council on Environmental Quality (Washington, D.C.), p. 100.

21. Conservation Foundation, *State of the Environment*, p. 97.

22. Lawrence White, *The Regulation of Air Pollutant Emissions From Motor Vehicles* (Washington, D.C.: The American Enterprise Institute, 1982), p. 55.

that had been issued; an ineffective enforcement system; and a scientific approach to standard setting that was unrealistic, costly, and in need of reform.

Not all of these difficulties can be laid at the door of the EPA. It is true that the agency's staff has generally chosen more, rather than less, detail and complexity in writing regulations, and this no doubt accounts for part of the delay in issuing standards. Moreover, compliance and enforcement issues have been given too little time and too few resources throughout the EPA's brief history. Nevertheless, Congress bears a large share of the responsibility for the problems with environmental regulation. Congress has passed enabling statutes containing unrealistic deadlines and an unnecessary degree of specificity with respect to the standards that the agency must issue. And by providing virtually no guidance as to what is meant by an "ample" or an "adequate" margin of safety, an "adverse" health effect, or an "economically achievable" emissions reduction, Congress has all but guaranteed that most EPA rules will be tested in court. Finally, by prohibiting consideration of costs in the setting of certain important standards, Congress has paved the way for rules that are not at all cost-effective.

A Blueprint for a Reagan Program

After the 1980 election, the Reagan administration might have established a policy direction for the 1980s that would appeal to its principal constituencies while not alarming those who view environmental policy as a crucial federal responsibility. Annual pollution control costs had risen steadily throughout the 1970s to more than $40 billion, and there was some evidence that the slowdown in productivity growth had been exacerbated by environmental policy.[23] Yet it was difficult to show that the EPA's policies had had a measurable effect on environmental quality. Clearly, there should have been some return on expenditures on the order of $40 billion per year.

The Reagan administration might have been expected to bemoan the absence of solid progress against environmental degradation after the expenditure of scores of billions of dollars. A major effort to find out whether or not the environmental programs adopted in the 1970s were working well

---

23. Edward Denison, "Effects of Selected Changes in the Institutional and Human Environment Upon Output per Unit of Input," *Survey of Current Business* (January 1978), pp. 21–44. See also, Robert Haveman and Gregory Christainsen, "Environmental Regulations and Productivity Growth," in Henry Peskin, Paul Portney, and Allen Kneese (eds.), *Environmental Regulation and the U.S. Economy* (Baltimore, Md.: Johns Hopkins University Press for Resources for the Future, 1981), pp. 55–76.

would have been attractive to environmentalists, EPA staff, and concerned citizens alike. Moreover, such a comprehensive review would have allowed the administration to buy the time it needed. Very few people, in or out of the administration, understood the depth and breadth of the problems that the EPA faced.[24] There could have been no better way of slowing the rate of growth of regulatory compliance costs than to announce that environmental policy would be reexamined before any new and possibly unproductive initiatives were launched.

The new administration, in short, would have been well advised to stress a critical reexamination of environmental policy rather than regulatory "relief."[25] Many citizens would view relief as a relaxation of environmental standards and thus as a threat to their health and welfare, especially in light of recent attention given to acid raid and to the improper disposal of hazardous wastes. But it would be difficult to object to a pause in initiatives while a major reexamination of existing policy was undertaken.

One might also have expected the administration's enthusiasm for supply-side economics—including the enhancement of incentives for savings and investment—to be reflected in its initial agenda for regulatory policies. Environmental policy would be especially important, given its contribution to the costs of building new industrial facilities. The new administration might have searched for ways to alleviate this government-supplied disincentive to new plant investment.

Finally, one might have expected the administration to search for ways of returning much of environmental policy to the states. Given the difficulties in monitoring and enforcing compliance from Washington, it could be argued that these responsibilities would be better dispatched by state and local governments. Where environmental problems clearly transcend national, state, or local borders (as with acid rain), and a national role is clearly appropriate, one might have expected the administration to ask for new powers or the strengthening of existing ones. The Reagan program for a new federalism could thus have been merged with the Reagan environmental policy.

These considerations suggest that an attractive environmental agenda for an incoming administration would have included an increase in the staff and

---

24. In addition to its responsibilities under the Clear Air Act, the Clean Water Act, the Resource Conservation and Recovery Act, and the Comprehensive Environmental Response, Compensation, and Liability Act (the Superfund), the EPA is empowered to regulate drinking water, toxic substances, and pesticides under the Safe Drinking Water Act, the Toxic Substances Control Act, and the Federal Insecticide, Fungicide, and Rodenticide Act.

25. For an excellent discussion of the administration's overall regulatory reform program, see George C. Eads and Michael Fix, *Relief or Reform? Reagan's Regulatory Dilemma* (Washington, D.C.: The Urban Institute Press, 1984).

capabilities of the EPA and the Executive Office of the President; increased expenditures for environmental monitoring and data collection; a search for new market incentives to substitute for inflexible regulatory approaches; a careful review of, and perhaps some changes in, standards issued prior to 1981; and a limited number of legislative initiatives designed to reduce the cost of environmental policy without increasing environmental risks.

Improved Analytical and Research Capabilities

Given the lack of solid analysis of the effects of the regulatory programs for which the EPA is responsible, the new administration might have launched a major effort to improve analytical capabilities at both the EPA and the White House (or at the Office of Management and Budget). This would have made it possible to understand the strengths and weaknesses of existing environmental programs. Although the EPA had one of the best analytical staffs among the regulatory agencies, it had never been able to provide retrospective assessments of regulatory policies while it was also trying to conduct complicated analyses of forthcoming new source performance standards, pretreatment standards, hazardous waste and toxic substance regulations, or ambient air quality standards.[26] Remedying this deficiency at the outset would have given the Reagan administration some badly needed credibility and would also have laid the groundwork for future initiatives. Expansion of the EPA's analytical and research staff would also have coincided with the position of some businessmen that it was the absence of "good science" or "good analysis" that led to unrealistic and costly regulation. Analytical expertise is inexpensive compared with the compliance costs generated by most environmental programs.

Improved Monitoring and Data Collection

Even a strong staff, however, would have faced a woeful lack of data on effluents, air and water quality, and hazardous waste and toxic chemical production, and would have had few useful measures of morbidity or of other damage caused by pollution. It is obviously impossible to estimate the effects of pollution on health and economic welfare if there are poor data on the rate of discharge of the major pollutants. Moreover, the objective of environmental policy must be to improve the quality of the air, water, and land; but the

---

26. Exceptions do exist. For example, the EPA had produced extensive analyses of the impacts of its regulations on five major industries (steel, copper, paper, utilities, and petroleum refining) between 1976 and 1978.

EPA has found it difficult to assemble data on current environmental quality. Finally, analysts must have better demographic data and information on human health in areas of differing environmental quality if they are to estimate the effects of pollution on health.

An immediate goal of an administration committed to rationalizing social regulation, therefore, would have been to improve environmental information. It is not sufficient to argue that available information is so bad that it cannot be used to defend current policies; the public is likely to support regulatory programs that offer some hope of reducing the problem, even if it cannot be sure of their success.

A Search for Market Incentives

The arrival of an administration committed to restoring work and savings incentives through supply-side tax reductions seemed to augur well for the use of market incentives in environmental, safety, and health regulation. The Carter administration had broken ground in this area with its "bubble" policy in air pollution regulation and its extension of the offset program begun under the Ford administration.[27] Under the ostensibly more market-oriented Reagan administration, one might have expected a major push for replacing or supplementing federal regulation with market incentives.

The agenda for extending market incentives might have included extending controlled trading of pollution abatement requirements to water pollution control and finding ways of extending trading in air pollution abatement requirements to new sources. The latter option might have required new legislation to permit trading in lieu of the stringent technology-based standards under Section 111 of the Clean Air Act,[28] but the act was due to be reauthorized in less than one year.

Given more time, the staff might have been instructed to examine the possibility of introducing market incentives into the control of air pollution from mobile sources (e.g., automobiles and trucks). The states' new vehicle inspection and maintenance programs were to be activated in 1982. Why not replace the pass-or-fail system of vehicle inspections with one in which cars with very high emission levels pay stiff annual fees while cars running cleanly are assessed very small fees or none at all? This might even have allowed

27. For a discussion of the implementation of bubbles and offsets, see Richard Liroff, *The Bubble Concept for Air Pollution Control: A Political and Administrative Perspective* (Washington, D.C.: The Conservation Foundation, 1981); and *Air Pollution Offsets: Trading, Banking, and Selling* (Washington, D.C.: The Conservation Foundation, 1982).

28. As a result of *Natural Resources Defense Council* v. *Gorsuch, et al.,*—685 F.(2d) 718 (D.C. Cir., August 17, 1982).

some reduction in the stringency of new-car standards, thereby helping the recovery of the automobile industry and the more rapid replacement of older, more polluting vehicles.

Reconsideration of Previous Standards

The improvement of staff analytical capabilities could have permitted a limited reexamination of existing standards as early as 1981. The rush to issue standards in the last days of the Carter administration was not particularly concentrated in the EPA, but examples of hasty or poor judgment might well have been found there. Standards governing the disposal of hazardous wastes and new source standards for major categories of air polluters would have been obvious candidates; so too would have been new source standards for electric utilities,[29] prevention of significant deterioration (PSD) standards, registration requirements for pesticides or reviews of new chemicals, and new source standards for major water pollutants.

Legislative Changes

Because many problems in environmental policy originate in complex, overly ambitious statutes, legislative change should have been high on the administration's agenda. The Clean Air Act was due for reauthorization in September 1981. Because it was arguably the single most important regulatory law passed in the 1970s, and because it typified many unfortunate aspects of environmental, safety, and health regulation, the Clean Air Act was an obvious candidate for careful review and amendment. The Clean Water Act was also on the legislative calendar. Even newer statutes, such as the Resource Conservation and Recovery Act or the Toxic Substances Control Act, might have been selected for possible modification.

In each case, the administration might have attempted to draft amendments that would allow greater use of flexible market incentives; reduce the procedural complexity of the EPA's administration of the statute; relieve undue burdens on new investment; restructure priorities toward the more dangerous environmental hazards; and provide incentives for state monitoring and enforcement. In both the Clean Air and Clean Water Acts, one might have expected proposed amendments expressly allowing the trading of pollution permits between new and old sources. For both acts, changes in legislative language would have assisted movement toward plant-wide pollution reduc-

---

29. See Bruce A. Ackerman and William J. Hassler, *Clean Coal/Dirty Air* (New Haven: Yale University Press, 1981), for a discussion of this regulatory fiasco.

tion requirements, and a change in emphasis from conventional, nonhazardous pollutants to toxic or hazardous pollutants might have been accomplished by amendment. And each statute might have been amended to give more authority to the states—a change consistent with the Reagan administration's concern for a new federalism.

Although these suggestions might have appealed to the ideological conservatives in the Reagan administration, they may not have been what the administration's business constituency wanted. There is little demand for economic efficiency or for the manipulation of market incentives in the business world. Some might suggest that businesses simply want special treatment or relief from standards they perceive to be onerous without a fundamental restructuring of federal policy. As private tort suits become more common, particularly cases centering on asbestos and hazardous waste, businesses might want the protection implicit in federal standards administered by probusiness officials.

It would be naive to suggest that the Reagan administration did not feel these pressures; but it would have been possible, in the early days, for the administration to have combined its search for short-run regulatory relief with a longer-term program designed to bring greater efficiency and less intrusiveness to federal environmental policy.

The Reagan Record on Environmental Protection

It is disappointing to compare the preceding agenda with the performance of the Reagan administration in environmental protection. This disappointment stems from mistaken priorities and missed opportunities. The administration's initial appointments to the EPA, certain budgetary and policy initiatives, and the impression left by the administration's activities have made Reagan's failure to correct the problems he inherited in environmental regulation inevitable.

Regulatory Appointments

Given the sweeping responsibilities of the EPA and the substantial problems that existed in attempting to fulfill them, the administration faced a choice. It could either appoint an EPA leadership drawn from the narrow fraternity of those familiar with the complex regulatory, scientific, and political issues at the agency, or one composed of strong managers who could draw on the agency's expertise while moving in a direction consistent with the Reagan program. It chose neither. The administration's choices for the top two positions at the EPA were curious indeed. Anne M. Gorsuch (later Burford), a lawyer from Colorado with no Washington experience and little substantive experience with environmental issues apart from that gathered as a member of the Colorado state legislature, became administrator; and the dean of a New Mexico engineering school, John Hernandez, became deputy administrator. Neither had the extensive managerial or governmental experience that would suggest that they could successfully lead a controversial agency in a time of change.

Neither position was filled in the first three months of the Reagan term, forcing the EPA to operate without clear, decisive policy guidance. This made it difficult to design new policies or solve old problems. It was also impossible to construct a legislative agenda without someone firmly in charge.

This might not have brought disaster if the new leadership had sought the cooperation of the established EPA staff. The appointment of inexperienced persons with little knowledge of the fields and issues they inherit is hardly a new phenomenon in Washington. But such appointees must either bring experienced staff or use the existing staff of their organizations well. The new leadership at the EPA instead went out of its way to suggest that the EPA bureaucracy was a large part of the agency's problem. Groups outside the agency prepared ''hit lists'' of supposedly pro-environmental EPA employees and the new leadership appeared to respond to them by, for example, replacing several members of the EPA Science Advisory Board. Many senior employees left, while others became resentful and distrustful of the new team.

The administration's appointments to other top positions at EPA brought further trouble. For the most part, the appointees were drawn from large corporations, the lawyers representing these firms, and Washington lobbyists. Most were people with no public reputation; few had much knowledge of the area they were to oversee or independent standing within the administration. These appointments, late as they were, combined with the administration's emphasis on regulatory relief to give many the impression that the new EPA leadership was meant to eviscerate the nation's environmental policies.

Two of the top appointees (the newly created associate administrators) resigned within three months; most of the rest of Reagan's EPA management team resigned or were dismissed early in 1983. Meanwhile, six congressional committees were investigating the EPA, documents were shredded, the administrator was held to be in contempt of Congress for refusing to turn over subpoenaed documents, and the behavior of a number of other agency officials was under scrutiny. A sorry spectacle, indeed.

Absence of Legislative Initiatives

The environmental statutes that require technology-based standards for controlling air pollution, water pollution, and solid wastes are highly complex; and many are also so ambitious as to be unenforceable. If the new administration was to reform environmental policy in a fundamental way, the statutes themselves would have to be changed.

Because there had been limited experience with the laws pertaining to toxic substances, hazardous wastes, and the Superfund, they were not likely candidates for fundamental change. On the other hand, reauthorization of the Clean Air Act was due within nine months of Reagan's inauguration and the deadline for reauthorizing the Clean Water Act was 1982. These two dates provided a clear opportunity for the administration to set a new agenda for air and water pollution policy.

Because of the delay in filling the top positions at EPA, it was summer 1981 before the Reagan EPA could turn to reauthorization of the Clean Air Act. By this time, the lobbying battle had heated up substantially. The Business Roundtable, the U.S. Chamber of Commerce, former officials of the EPA, and various environmental groups were trading accusations about possible changes in ambient air quality standards, PSD policy, automobile emissions standards, and statutory deadlines. Environmentalists saw many attempts to modify the act as assaults on the fundamental purposes of air pollution policy. Because of the difficulties facing the automobile industry, some were arguing that provisions of the act pertaining to stationary sources should be left more or less intact so that relief from the carbon monoxide and nitrogen dioxide emissions standards could be granted the auto makers.

The new EPA leadership worked on drafting proposed legislation, but it abandoned the effort in August, offering instead a set of eleven "principles" by which the administration would be guided in supporting amendments to the Clean Air Act.[30] These principles included keeping the statutory language calling for health-based ambient standards, revising the new source provisions for coal-fired electric utilities, relaxing automobile emissions standards, and easing statutory deadlines for achieving air quality goals. With little White House or EPA leadership and a contentious congressional spirit on environmental issues, no new legislation was passed in 1981, 1982, or 1983.

Similarly, the administration has not pressed for fundamental change in the Clean Water Act. Although there is evidence that the current policy has had little effect on water quality, no one—not the administration, nor the

---

30. Statement of EPA Administrator Anne M. Gorsuch, August 5, 1981.

business community, nor environmentalists—appears concerned.[31] The technology-based standards mandated by the act are likely to be inefficient and quite wasteful because they apply to all sources, regardless of the quality of the receiving water. Water quality regulation might be better, and it would make sense to return more of the standard-setting responsibilities to the states. This potentially happy link with the administration's new federalism has been ignored by the EPA and the White House.

The lack of initiatives for legislative change is not trivial. If environmental policy is to move from centralized standard-setting to more efficient and effective market incentives, legislative constraints must be removed. The Clean Air Act in particular has numerous provisions that limit the operation of transferable emissions reduction credits. The percentage reduction standard for new coal-fired power plants, the new source standards in nonattainment areas, and the emissions standards for hazardous air pollutants all limit trading of pollution control requirements that could reduce control costs without compromising (or, in some cases, while improving) air quality. The Clean Water Act's focus on technological standards rather than water quality management similarly limits the use of marketable incentives. Small changes in each statute might provide a great deal of regulatory "relief" without increasing public exposure to pollution.

The Use of Economic Incentives

Perhaps the most notable accomplishment of the Carter administration's EPA was the introduction of economic incentives into air pollution policy. The Ford administration had introduced "offsets" into requirements for new source construction in areas that did not meet ambient air quality standards. A new source had to purchase pollution reductions—offsets—from other sources in the area so that the new source could be built without increasing local pollution. The offsets had to be for *more* emissions than those that the new source would generate, thereby facilitating the "reasonable further progress" toward improving local air quality required by the Clean Air Act.

The Carter administration formalized and extended the offset requirement into an emissions trading policy, allowing trades between sources at a plant and between plants in the same area as well as existing and new sources. Such "bubble" trading allowed a more economic assumption of pollution abatement: sources where pollution control was costly reduced abatement, while sources where it was less costly increased abatement. Unfortunately,

31. See Henry M. Peskin, "Preserving Illusions—The Clean Water Act After Ten Years," *Resources*, no. 72 (February 1983), p. 12.

the EPA has been unable to extend the trading concept fully to new sources because the courts have insisted that "reasonable further progress" toward attainment in nonattainment areas requires strict, technology-based new source performance standards.

During the Carter administration, attempts to introduce offset trading in water pollution policy were stymied by opposition from members of Congress and high-ranking EPA officials. With change in both the administration and the Senate, one might have expected new momentum for marketable rights in this area, but the new administration warmed very slowly to the concept.

The Reagan EPA did not advance the concept of economic incentives at all for several months. Despite efforts by the agency's analytical staff, the new administrator and her appointees appeared to be rather hostile to offset trading, either out of ignorance of its advantages or fear of political backlash. Instead, they were firmly committed to much stricter standards for new sources of air pollution than for existing sources despite the obvious effect of such an approach on new investment—and even on pollution in the near term.

In 1982 the Reagan EPA made its first substantive attempt to advance marketable pollution permits, proposing a trading policy that would guide future regulatory decisions.[32] This policy statement followed an earlier decision that would permit a new source to escape new source review in both nonattainment and PSD areas if there were to be no net increase in emissions.[33] This would have allowed a firm to avoid a costly review of an installation undergoing a modification as long as emissions were reduced elsewhere in the plant. This policy was, however, struck down by the D.C. Circuit Court as not applicable in nonattainment areas.[34] The decision is on appeal.

A second belated effort to promote rationality in pollution control appeared in new effluent guidelines for the steel industry. The industry will be allowed to adjust control responsibilities across sources in a plant, much as happens in a "bubble" for air pollution.

More progress has recently been made on this front. The EPA has instituted a lead trading policy that enables refiners to reduce the lead content of gasoline at the least expensive sources. According to the agency, 10 percent of all the lead now used in gasoline has been traded among sources. The EPA has also implemented a limited emissions-averaging program for mobile sources—a kind of bubble policy available to the makers of automobiles and other vehicles. This averaging, limited to light-duty diesel particulate matter, may be extended soon to heavy-duty diesel nitrogen oxides emissions. In

---

32. 47 *Federal Register* 15076-15086.
33. 46 *Federal Register* 50766-50771.
34. See note 28.

spite of these recent and encouraging developments, however, the agency has yet to embrace a legislative proposal to allow trades between new and existing sources of air pollution or to extend the bubble policy to water pollution control. Although such proposals will be controversial, they are also necessary if pollution control is to be made less expensive and less biased against the construction of new industrial facilities.

The EPA Budget

The Reagan administration has been very effective in slashing the budget of the Environmental Protection Agency. This may reflect a desire to accomplish two goals at once—reducing the rate of growth of federal spending on all domestic programs, and scaling back federal regulatory activity. It is clear that the first of these goals was seen as a means of accomplishing the second. Along with administrative changes in regulatory oversight,[35] budget reductions have undoubtedly affected environmental regulation.

The Congressional Budget Office has recently analyzed budget trends for EPA operating programs in air quality, water quality, hazardous wastes, and toxic substances.[36] In 1983 these four programs accounted for about 60 percent of the agency's operating budget, and may be taken to indicate trends at the agency as a whole. The 1984 budget request for these four operating programs is 19 percent lower in real terms than 1983 spending (see table 1). The decline in spending for water quality programs would amount to 33 percent if the administration's budget request is approved by Congress, with the proposed reductions for air quality, hazardous waste, and toxics being 14 percent, 10 percent, and 9 percent, respectively.

Comparing the fiscal year 1981 and proposed 1984 budgets for the EPA gives a better picture of the overall changes in the agency's budget during the Reagan administration.[37] Over this period, the budget for the EPA's four major operating programs has fallen by 44 percent in real terms. The largest declines have been in the water quality area, where the budget has fallen by

---

    35. See George C. Eads and Michael Fix, "Regulatory Policy," in John L. Palmer and Isabel V. Sawhill (eds.), *The Reagan Experiment* (Washington, D.C.: The Urban Institute Press, 1982), pp. 129–156.

    36. U.S. Congressional Budget Office, "The Environmental Protection Agency: Overview of the Proposed 1984 Budget," Staff Working Paper (April 1983).

    37. The changes are even more dramatic if they are measured from a fiscal year 1980 base. However, actual obligations in fiscal year 1981, although no doubt influenced to some extent by the Reagan administration, are probably best attributed to the Carter administration. President Reagan's inauguration came four months into fiscal year 1981 and most of that year was over before the full cabinet was assembled. Interestingly, the data show the beginnings of a drop in funding for the EPA before the Reagan team took over.

TABLE 1

BUDGET AND STAFF CHANGES IN SELECTED EPA OPERATING PROGRAMS, FISCAL
YEARS 1981–1984

| | Budget Levels | | | | | | |
| | Actual obligations | | | Budget authority | | Percentage change | |
Program Area	1980	1981	1982	1983[a]	1984[b]	1983–84	1981–84
	(Millions of 1982 dollars)						
Water quality	400	341	251	207	138	−33	−59
Air quality	336	252	230	204	175	−14	−31
Hazardous waste	128	151	111	112	100	−10	−34
Toxic substances	104	100	82	67	61	−9	−40
Total	968	844	674	590	474	−19	−44

| | Staff Levels | | | | Percentage change | |
| | Number of employees[c] | | | | | |
Water quality	2,781	2,273	1,953	1,663	−15	−40
Air quality	1,754	1,576	1,375	1,351	−2	−23
Hazardous waste	726	586	643	626	−3	−14
Toxic substances	716	634	627	606	−3	−15
Total	5,977	5,069	4,598	4,246	−8	−29

SOURCE: Congressional Budget Office, "The Environmental Protection Agency: Overview of the Proposed 1984 Budget," p. 5 (based on data obtained from EPA). Data for 1980 supplied separately by Congressional Budget Office.

NOTE: Percentage changes were calculated from annual budget figures before rounding and, therefore, represent actual differences. Budget figures in the table have been rounded to the nearest million and may not produce the same percentage difference.

a. Estimated.
b. Requested.
c. Permanent, full-time employees only.

nearly 60 percent, and the toxic substances program, where the proposed budget is 40 percent below its 1981 level. Clearly, in these four major areas the Reagan administration has pursued a steady policy of reducing the resources available to the EPA. These budget reductions have brought with them predictable reductions in full-time employees at the agency. According to the Congressional Budget Office, the number of full-time employees in these program areas will have fallen 29 percent from 1981 if the 1984 budget request is granted.

Budgets can be analyzed by function—in this case, by pollution abatement and control, enforcement, and research and development—as well as by program area. According to the Congressional Budget Office, the real percentage declines in EPA spending between 1981 and the 1984 proposal have been fairly evenly distributed among these three functions; in real terms, abatement and control has declined by 46 percent, enforcement by 39 percent, and research and development by 38 percent (see table 2). Proposed spending for these combined functions will fall by nearly one-fifth even measured against expected spending in 1983. Given the very serious problems with compliance and enforcement, the quality of the data on which air quality and other standards are to be based, and the quality of monitoring data, it is hard to see how budget reductions in the latter two areas will do anything but exacerbate already considerable difficulties.

The administration favors transferring to the states the responsibility of running many heretofore federally managed environmental programs, but federal assistance for such purposes is being reduced. Between 1983 and 1984 federal assistance to the states for air and water quality programs and hazardous

TABLE 2

TOTAL BUDGET AND STAFF CHANGES IN ACTIVITIES OF EPA OPERATING
PROGRAMS, FISCAL YEARS 1981–1984

	Budget Levels				Percentage change	
	Actual obligations		Budget authority			
Function	1981	1982	1983[a]	1984[b]	1983–84	1981–84
	(Millions of 1982 dollars)					
Abatement and control	584	426	397	313	−21	−46
Enforcement	82	68	49	50	+4	−39
Research and development	178	180	144	111	−23	−38
Total	844	674	590	474	−19	−44
	Staff Levels				Percentage change	
	Number of employees[c]					
Abatement and control	3,364	2,761	2,663	2,445	−8	−27
Enforcement	1,513	1,307	1,011	990	−2	−35
Research and development	1,100	1,001	924	811	−12	−26
Total	5,977	5,609	4,598	4,246	−8	−29

SOURCE: Congressional Budget Office, "The Environmental Protection Agency: Overview of the Proposed 1984 Budget," p. 3 (based on data obtained from EPA).

NOTE: Percentage changes were calculated from annual budget figures before rounding and, therefore, represent actual differences. Budget figures in the table have been rounded to the nearest million and may not produce the same percentage differences.

a. Estimated.
b. Requested.
c. Permanent, full-time employees only.

waste control efforts would fall 28 percent in real terms under the administration budget, from $321 million to $230 million. Federal aid to states for environmental purposes would decline by 44 percent from 1981 levels under the proposed budget. The states have made it clear that they will be unable to match reductions in federal spending with increases in local spending.[38] Because most environmental and compliance monitoring is undertaken by the states, the quality of these activities is likely to decline rather than improve. Thirty-six states reported in a 1981 survey that they would reduce their ambient air quality monitoring proportionately to the reduction in federal support of state environmental activities.[39]

There is some evidence that the reduction in funds to the states may already be affecting compliance and enforcement. Recently, GAO surveyed 531 major industrial and municipal water polluters in six states and found that 82 percent had exceeded their permitted discharge levels at least once during an 18-month period beginning in October 1980.[40] Fully 31 percent of these offenders exceeded their permit levels by 50 percent or more for at least four consecutive months. During this same period formal enforcement actions by the EPA declined by 41 percent (continuing a trend that had begun in 1977).

The proposed 1984 budget for research and development represents a decline of 23 percent from 1983 and a 38 percent decline from 1981 levels; however, this reduction is not distributed evenly. Expenditures for the salaries of employees and associated operating costs would be about 20 percent lower in 1984 than in 1981. Funding for outside and longer-term research—necessary to identify possible problems for which no regulatory apparatus exists—will be cut much more severely. The decline from 1983 to 1984 is 24 percent; however, it is part of a three-year effort that would see extramural research in these four program areas fall by nearly half from 1981 levels. One must conclude that the scientific basis for environmental quality standards will deteriorate sharply; and understanding of possible new environmental problems, as well as knowledge about how current programs address existing problems, can be expected to diminish under the administration's budget.

The administration has asked for a substantial increase in budget authority for the Hazardous Substances Response Trust Fund (the ''Superfund''). The Superfund would receive $310 million in 1984, 41 percent more in real terms

---

38. National Governors' Association, *The State of the States: Management of Environmental Programs in the 1980s* (Washington, D.C.: National Governors' Association, 1982), pp. 1–4.

39. Ibid., p. 10.

40. U.S. General Accounting Office, *Wastewater Dischargers Are Not Complying With EPA Pollution Control Permits*, Report RCED-84-53, December 2, 1983.

than expected 1983 spending, and nearly six times as much as was appropriated to the fund in 1981 when it began. This money would presumably be used to initiate clean-up actions at some of the National Priority Sites, locations at which abandoned hazardous wastes are posing health and other risks to nearby residents.

It is not true, of course, that all budget reductions are unfortunate. For example, this administration has virtually eliminated the EPA's noise control program. Although prolonged exposure to loud noise can cause serious problems, controlling noise can probably best be handled locally; the problem seldom crosses jurisdictional lines, and reducing the federal role in noise pollution seems quite appropriate. Similarly, as regulatory responsibilities are met in air or water quality programs, one might reasonably expect an eventual reduction in resources allocated to these programs. The completion of certain standard-setting activities can be used to make a case for some of these reductions. However, this is an insufficient basis for the reductions in the EPA budget that the administration has proposed. Far too little is known about who is discharging what, about what the real level of environmental quality is, and about the best means of ensuring compliance on the part of those violating permits.

Additionally, the hazardous waste and toxic substances programs have yet to get under way although the enabling statutes were passed in 1976. There is yet virtually no information on how these programs will work. More seriously, there is real reason to question the approach that Congress and the EPA have taken to hazardous waste and toxic substance control, suggesting that some resources might be devoted to developing alternative approaches. This is hardly a propitious time to cut back the resources available to the EPA for hazardous waste and toxic substance management.

Moreover, one has to view the EPA budget from the perspective of the true annual cost of environmental regulation in the United States. The United States now spends more than $40 billion per year to comply with federal environmental regulations; the operating budget of the EPA, at about $1 billion per year, accounts for no more than 2 percent or 3 percent of this total. Increasing the EPA budget—particularly that devoted to agency analytical capability, improved ambient and compliance monitoring, and long- and short-term research—might make it possible to reduce the total resources devoted to environmental protection each year while maintaining or improving the quality of the environment.

Construction Grants.   This discussion of the EPA budget would be incomplete without some mention of the construction grants program mandated by Title II of the Clean Water Act. Federal expenditures to help subsidize the cost of building municipal sewage treatment plants have always dwarfed the operating budget of the EPA; annual expenditures have been as large as $4 billion, although they have been approximately $2.4 billion for the past four years. This was the amount requested by the Reagan administration for 1984.

The construction grants program is one EPA program about which there has been broad agreement among environmentalists and economists: many bemoan the very uncertain and uneven contribution the program has made to water quality, especially in view of its cost.[41] The essence of the problem is that although the program does cover a substantial share of the cost of building a sewage treatment plant (75 percent in most cases), it cannot be used to cover the costs of operating and maintaining the plants that are built. Communities have sometimes built very sophisticated and expensive plants only to find that they cannot afford to operate or maintain them properly. Some plants have been abandoned almost on completion.

The ambiguous effects of the construction grants program on water quality make it a likely target for substantial budget cuts, and the Reagan administration has in fact spent less than prior ones on the program. The administration has also proposed amendments to the Clean Water Act that would reduce the federal share of the cost of constructing new waste treatment plants, and it has issued regulations designed to ensure that localities building new plants could afford to operate and maintain them. However, the Office of Management and Budget added $400 million to the EPA's original request for $2.0 billion for construction grants in 1984—while trying to force cuts of $104 million in operating expenses on top of the EPA's already substantially reduced operating budget.

Although this behavior is difficult to explain from the standpoint of environmental cost-effectiveness, it is intelligible from another perspective. The construction grants program has become one of the largest public works program in this nation's history, pumping more than $22 billion into new construction between 1972 and 1981. Expanding this program when the unemployment rate was above 10 percent was an attractive proposition: it offered new jobs without requiring the admission that unemployment had reached a problem level.

The budget cuts proposed for the EPA should be viewed in the broader context of overall federal budget policy. Between 1981 and 1984, the administration tried to reduce, or slow the growth of the budgets of most federal agencies. On the other hand, although the EPA was not alone in facing proposed reductions, it was (along with the Office of Surface Mining and the

---

41. For a discussion of this program see Allen V. Kneese and Charles Schultze, *Pollution, Prices and Public Policy* (Washington, D.C.: Brookings Institution, 1975).

Consumer Product Safety Commission) singled out for much larger cuts than were other federal agencies.

Regulatory Backlogs

The Reagan administration has made progress in reducing the backlog of decisions and unfinished rules it inherited, especially in the area of effluent guidelines for industrial water polluters. When the administration took office in January 1981, revised effluent guidelines had been promulgated only for the timber industry; twenty-seven other industries were awaiting rules. In May 1981, guidelines largely completed by the Carter EPA were promulgated for the iron and steel industry. Final rules have since been issued for eleven other industries and proposed for another ten industrial categories. In view of the increased resources devoted to the program, the EPA will apparently meet the schedule it set for itself of finishing the program by 1984. Much of the analysis supporting these effluent guidelines was completed in a previous administration, but the Reagan EPA committed itself to making proposals and finalizing rules, and for this, it deserves credit.

There has been less progress in the air quality program, but here, too, there are bright spots; for example, the EPA has reduced the backlog of proposed changes in State Implementation Plans (SIP). By April 1983 the EPA had processed 97 percent of the 643 proposed SIP changes it inherited in January 1981, and was processing proposals faster than new ones were coming in. Of the 289 SIP actions awaiting approval in April 1983, EPA was on schedule with 252 (or 87 percent of them).[42] If care was taken in the processing of these proposals (and this is an important "if"), progress has been made in this area.

In other aspects of air quality management, however, the record is dreary. Only one revision to a National Ambient Air Quality Standard has been proposed or finalized since the Reagan administration took office, although the Carter EPA had left a proposed revision to the carbon monoxide standard that had only to be reviewed, perhaps modified, and made final. Similarly, much of the groundwork for revisions to the nitrogen dioxide and sulfur dioxide standards had been done when the administration came in, but no proposals have been made.

The EPA has also been very slow in issuing New Source Performance Standards for major industrial categories. According to a priority list established in 1979, the EPA was to have promulgated New Source Performance Standards for all listed industries by August 1982. Yet there are still many

---

42. Information supplied by the Environmental Protection Agency.

industries for which there are no such standards, including those that use coal to fire their steam boilers. And no new hazardous air pollutants have been listed since 1980, nor have any regulations been issued in the past three years—no improvement at all since the end of 1980.

Very little progress can be reported in regulatory activity under the Resource Conservation and Recovery Act. Interim final regulations were issued in July of 1982 for landfills and surface storage impoundments, but these regulations represented a significant relaxation of similar rules proposed under the Carter administration. Permitting under the RCRA has been very slow; only one permit for the treatment, storage, or disposal of hazardous waste was issued in 1981, and only four were issued in 1982.[43] The EPA has identified some 10,000 sites that will eventually need such permits. At this rate it will be next millenium before this permitting process is complete.

Toxic substance policy is in a slightly better state. Although there has been no progress comparable to that in the effluent guideline and SIP areas, the administration has secured some voluntary agreements from industries to test certain chemicals, avoiding the "notice-and-comment" approach that must be used under the formal regulatory process. According to the Congressional Budget Office, the EPA intends to propose or promulgate about thirty such formal test rules in 1984.[44] This seems highly unlikely; only two such test rules have been proposed since 1976, when the Toxic Substances Control Act was passed, and none has been finalized. The backlog of applications for new pesticide registrations has been reduced, although serious questions have been raised about the care with which these applications were reviewed. Some concern has also been expressed about how carefully applications for reregistration of existing pesticides have been examined.

Policy Controversies

Apart from budgetary matters, there have been very few significant policy changes in the Reagan EPA. Most of the public controversy that swirled around Administrator Gorsuch during her tenure—charges of conflict of interest, partisan politics, and a general pro-business attitude—resulted from the EPA's handling of the hazardous waste program under RCRA or the cleaning up of hazardous waste dumps under the Superfund.

The hazardous waste program mandated under the RCRA is extremely ambitious. It requires the EPA to establish a tracking system for all listed hazardous wastes; a regulatory system for all treatment, storage, and disposal

---

43. Congressional Budget Office, "The Environmental Protection Agency. . . ," p. 31.
44. Ibid., p. 38.

facilities (TSDFs); and a permit system for all new facilities, and eventually for existing facilities. In a recent study, the Office of Technology Assessment remarked on the "simplicity" of this approach, but then noted that implementation has been characterized by "delay, false starts, frequent policy reversal, and litigation."[45] Clearly, attempting to regulate every major TSDF is neither simple nor politically straightforward.

Originally, the RCRA provided that no TSDF could operate without a permit after 1978, while existing facilities could operate under interim status until final standards were issued by the EPA. In May 1980 the Carter administration issued the interim status regulations for all TSDFs that would govern all facilities until they obtained permits, and interim standards governing the permitting of new facilities were issued in January 1981. Final technical standards, which are to supersede the interim standards as facilities obtain final permits, have been promulgated for most but not all TSDFs. Standards for underground storage or treatment facilities have not been promulgated, and the standards for land disposal facilities were substantially modified by the Reagan administration. But these standards do not govern any facilities until the permits are issued, and the permitting process could easily take another five to ten years.[46]

In July 1982 the Reagan administration issued its final standards for land disposal facilities, substituting performance standards in part for the Carter administration's proposed design standards. The revised standards rely heavily on site-specific groundwater monitoring, but critics contend that such monitoring is likely to be inadequate.[47] Given the substantial risk that hazardous liquids will eventually migrate through their containers or the landfill liners, monitoring may be quite important in protecting the groundwater from which drinking water is drawn—but the EPA does not even require monitoring in some cases. Moreover, given the large number of such facilities and the EPA's inability to supervise monitoring sites for air and water pollution, one must be skeptical about EPA's ability to monitor compliance with land disposal performance standards.

Several features of the debate over land disposal facilities are particularly noteworthy. First, it is another example of environmentalists' preference for

45. Office of Technology Assessment, *Technologies and Management Strategies for Hazardous Waste Control* (Washington, D.C.: March 1983).

46. Lawrence Mosher, "EPA Still Doesn't Know the Dimensions of Nation's Hazardous Waste Problem," *National Journal* (April 16, 1983), p. 797.

47. Office of Technology Assessment, *Technologies and Management Strategies for Hazardous Waste Control*. In the EPA's first check on groundwater monitoring under the Resource Conservation and Recovery Act, as many as 60 percent of hazardous waste disposal facilities failed to comply with the monitoring requirements. See *Air and Water Pollution Report* (March 21, 1983), p. 105.

design standards. A performance standard is likely to be more efficient than a design standard, but only if it can be monitored and enforced. Similar debates have raged for a decade in air and water pollution policy.

Second, solid-waste management seems to offer state and local authorities a comparative advantage, and under the RCRA, states may adopt their own programs and assume primary responsibility if they meet minimum federal standards. The Reagan EPA, however, has actively discouraged such a development by moving to eliminate federal funding of state programs, a curious initiative for an administration devoted to a new federalism.

Finally, much of the controversy swirling around the RCRA program at EPA had to do with the EPA's handling of landfill regulations. In 1982 Administrator Gorsuch suspended a ban on the dumping of liquids in landfills. At that time, James Sanderson, Gorsuch's apparent choice for associate administrator for policy and resource management, was serving simultaneously as a consultant to the EPA and to a solid-waste firm in Colorado. His client in Colorado apparently dumped thousands of barrels of liquids into landfills during the eighteen days after Gorsuch lifted the ban and before congressional protests forced her to reimpose it.[48] This simply served to confirm the distrust of EPA that had developed over the previous eighteen months.

Charges of political favoritism were nowhere more evident than in the administration's handling of the Superfund program, which had been designed to provide the mechanism and the funding for cleaning up abandoned hazardous waste facilities. Congress had instructed the EPA to list at least 400 priority sites for the initial phase of the Superfund program. EPA published this list in stages, beginning in October 1981 and finishing with a list of 419 sites in December 1982.

The Superfund program was controversial from the outset. The Reagan EPA has attempted to negotiate clean-up programs with those apparently responsible for the sites rather than using enforcement orders and court actions, and clean-up action has begun at very few sites. Through April 1983, EPA had succeeded in gaining commitments from responsible parties to clean up only 14 of the 419 designated sites. Five sites have been cleaned up, and work is beginning on another eighty-nine.[49] The Superfund, derived mostly from taxes on natural gas and petroleum use in manufacturing, is now thought adequate for cleaning up only 170 sites.[50] States have been reluctant to participate because they must pay 10 percent of the cost of cleaning up privately owned abandoned dumps and 50 percent of the cost at public dumps.

---

48. Lawrence Mosher, "EPA Still Doesn't Know," p. 798.
49. Ibid., p. 799.
50. Ibid.

The Superfund controversy involves political favoritism as well. For example, the former head of the program, Rita Lavelle, participated in discussions concerning a site in California into which her immediate past employer, Aerojet General, had dumped wastes. This led to her dismissal and eventual conviction—and it also deflected attention from the real problems of managing a large, controversial program involving the currently emotional problem of abandoned waste sites.

Another emotional issue embroiled in political controversy was the role of lead in gasoline. With the trend towards unleaded gasoline caused by the use of catalytic converters on virtually all new cars since the mid-1970s, the average lead content in gasoline will fall. But there continues to be concern for long-term effects of lead poisoning in children, even if it is difficult to link this lead contamination to gasoline.

The EPA had issued regulations phasing out lead in motor fuel under the Carter administration: refiners were to reduce their fuel's average content to 0.5 grams of lead per gallon, and small refiners were given two years to comply. (This strange exception led to a predictable result: small firms were able to buy gasoline and sell it with a higher lead content than large refiners.) In 1981, the EPA proposed to extend the deadline for small refiners and to exempt large refiners from the standard for gasoline sold in nonurban areas.[51]

This proposal sparked a controversy that was heightened by a much-publicized meeting between Administrator Gorsuch and officials of a small refinery in which she allegedly assured them that she would not enforce the lead phasedown requirements on the company after October 1982.[52] Although this episode did not result in any legal action, it obviously affected the administrator and the regulatory watchdogs at the Office of Management and Budget. The EPA suddenly changed course in August 1982 and resumed the lead phasedown program. The agency announced a new standard of 1.10 grams per gallon in leaded gasoline in October 1982[53] and extended the small-refiner exemption only until July 1, 1983. This mollified environmentalists while it gave the politically influential small refiners another eight months to comply.

Summary

The Reagan administration had a golden opportunity to launch a major assessment of past environmental policies and to lay the groundwork for a

---

51. 47 Federal Register 4812.

52. Jane Stein, "Warning from Health Experts: Anti-Lead Drive is Running Out of Gas," *National Journal* (June 5, 1982), p. 1007.

53. 47 Federal Register 49322.

new approach to environmental policy—one making expanded use of economic incentives. Disappointingly, the administration has neglected the first opportunity altogether and has only recently begun, cautiously, to extend the domain of market-based approaches to environmental protection.

There are several reasons for this. First, the Reagan EPA was initially saddled with a management team that had little substantive experience in environmental protection and was also suspicious of the EPA staff members on whom they might have depended for expertise. The fates of many appointees did much to damage the reputation of an agency that had previously been highly regarded for its professionalism. In part because of the flaws of this team, the administration has also failed to push for meaningful changes in any of the major statutes underlying air or water pollution control or the management of toxic substances or hazardous wastes. This reliance on administrative changes will make it easy for later administrations to reverse policy actions taken under Reagan.

The administration's preoccupation with reducing the EPA's budget has also greatly hampered the agency's effectiveness. Many opportunities that presented themselves to the administration at the EPA—an expanded monitoring network, improved analytical capabilities, increased delegation to the states— would have required more, not less, spending; but this conflicted with the administration's budget plan as well as its desire to use the EPA as a vehicle for regulatory relief rather than as a focus of regulatory reform.

A New Direction for Environmental Policy

The appointment of the experienced William Ruckelshaus to head the EPA has restored much of the credibility lost under his predecessor. Ruckelshaus has assembled a management team that has almost all of the qualities that were lacking in the initial appointments to the agency and is in a position to begin to do (in late 1983) what should have been attempted in 1981. Because of the new confidence that this group has won, and because Congress has consistently resisted cutting the EPA's budget to the extent requested by the administration, the agency's budget picture has even improved somewhat.

Unfortunately, it will be difficult to pursue necessary changes in environmental policy because of the ill will aroused by the Reagan administration's first appointees and the proximity of the 1984 election. It will still be useful to lay out an agenda for environmental policy in the years to come, an agenda worth pursuing by any administration.

The EPA must commit both analytical and financial resources to improving the network of ambient environmental quality monitors and individual source discharge monitors. There must be more air and water quality monitors across the country, as well as an improvement in the quality of the data each produces. More air pollution monitors would be required in the next several years in any case—the EPA is about to change the basis of the ambient air quality standard for particulates matter from total suspended particulate matter to finer particulate matter of 10 microns or less. More ozone and other types of monitors should be sited as well, especially in rural areas for which there are virtually no data now. There must be another basis for estimates of air-pollution-induced crop loss than the current monitored readings in metropolitan areas. Similarly, the EPA ought to increase dramatically the number of sulfate monitoring stations in both urban and rural areas. Not only are sulfates an important precursor of acid rain, but apparently they are also much more likely than sulfur dioxide to result in elevated morbidity and/or mortality rates.[54]

The need for improved water quality monitors is even more urgent. The EPA should seriously consider reviving and expanding its now-moribund National Water Quality Surveillance System. Failing that, the EPA might provide added resources to the U.S. Geological Survey for the National Stream Quality Accounting Network (NASQAN). The NASQAN system is currently the only thing approaching a comprehensive national water quality monitoring program; unfortunately, recent budget cuts have forced the Survey to reduce the frequency with which system data are collected and reported. Finally, it is time to consider establishing a national groundwater monitoring network. Groundwater provides 25 percent of all fresh water used in the United States each year.[55] It is too important a resource to go unobserved, especially in view of its possible contamination in heavily industrialized areas or, in some places, by chemical and other hazardous wastes.

More money must also be spent on enforcement. Stack or outfall tests, including more unannounced tests, must eventually replace site inspections as the principal means of determining compliance with air and water pollution regulations. There should also be some form of continuous monitoring, to provide information on how extensively standards are violated during shutdowns of pollution control equipment and subsequent "cold starts." Sources found to be in violation in one or more inspections should be inspected

---

54. See, for instance, Lester Lave and Eugene Seskin, *Air Pollution and Human Health* (Baltimore, Md.: Johns Hopkins University Press for Resources for the Future, 1977).

55. *Environmental Quality: 1980*, The Eleventh Annual Report of the Council on Environmental Quality (Washington, D.C., 1981), p. 83.

regularly to ensure that they are on a schedule that will bring them into compliance in a reasonable period of time. Recalcitrant sources ought to face certain and substantial penalties.

Funding such an improved effort should not be difficult. The EPA's annual expenditures for all air and water quality monitoring amount to less than $100 million (less than 0.3 percent of the total annual cost of complying with the regulations written in pursuit of these goals).[56] An additional $100 million would double the current effort (although more might be required if really substantial improvements are to be made). Congress might keep this in mind when considering possible enlargements in the EPA's budget. For fiscal year 1984, for example, it appears that the appropriation for EPA will be on the order of $1.15 billion, more than 20 percent higher than the administration's request.

Devoting additional money to improved monitoring and enforcement, would help in developing the capability to determine whether or not past efforts have proved effective. If they have not, it might well be time to pause and rethink this nation's approach to environmental protection over the past thirteen years. Barring substantially increased appropriations, resources ought to be redirected toward monitoring and enforcement—and given the rather poor record of the construction grants program, sums originally intended for this program might reasonably be among those redirected.

The EPA should forcefully expand the use of economic incentives in environmental policy. Although the Reagan EPA was slow to build on the efforts of the previous two administrations in this area, some progress has been made. Further progress will require a steady and unbending effort to advance the use of incentive mechanisms under the current statutes. This will necessarily be slow—it will not be easy to modify, much less reverse, a decade-long reliance on command-and-control regulation—but study after study has documented the savings in control costs that would result if pollution reduction takes place at sources with low control costs.[57]

There are several obvious areas where bubble- or offset-like mechanisms would be useful. Water pollution policy is ripe for such an innovation. Marketable discharge permits are already being used in Wisconsin to improve the

---

56. See Council on Environmental Quality, *Final Report of the Interagency Task Force on Environmental Data and Monitoring* (March 21, 1980), pp. 4–5.

57. The most important of these studies are discussed in Peter Bohm and Clifford S. Russell, "Comparative Analysis of Alternative Policy Instruments," unpublished manuscript. For an analysis of variations in marginal control costs both within and between industries regulated by the EPA, see "The Incremental Cost-Effectiveness of Selected EPA Regulations," draft report of Office of Planning and Management, U.S. Environmental Protection Agency (January 23, 1981).

efficiency of water pollution policy.[58] A national trading policy could be adopted administratively or built into the Clean Water Act. Every effort should be made to do so.

The EPA should also pursue more vigorously the extension of the offset policy to new sources of air pollution. The policy would allow new facilities to install less sophisticated, less expensive pollution control equipment than is now required if they secure further reductions in pollution from existing sources in the area. The savings that might result from a trading system that included new sources would be substantial,[59] especially where existing facilities—coal-fired power plants, steel mills, and other large sources—are virtually uncontrolled, while new plants are forced to meet very stringent emissions control requirements. In these cases, very large cost savings are possible while maintaining the same level of environmental quality.

There is, however, one important prerequisite for a well-functioning system of tradeable pollution permits: an accurate inventory of emissions from all sources of pollution. Without such a record, ''paper trades'' might take place, causing deterioriation of environmental quality and undermining support for the system. Although the EPA maintains such an inventory, the agency's figures do not inspire confidence—estimated national emissions for the years 1970 through 1978 differed in 1980 and 1982 reports from the EPA, even though both reports dealt with a period well in the past.[60] Developing an inventory that could form the basis of a legally enforceable system of tradeable rights will not be easy; but it is another area in which the commitment of additional resources would make possible an alternative approach to environmental protection that would more than recoup its cost.

There are a number of other problems that the EPA should address. First, the agency is woefully behind in a number of its responsibilities under the Clean Air Act. Perhaps this is because of the ambitious nature of the environmental laws; but the EPA still must make an effort to meet its statutory responsibilities. Standards for hazardous pollutants and new sources are incomplete. The National Ambient Air Quality Standards have not been revised

58. See Anthony S. Earl, ''Achieving Environmental Quality in the Face of Social, Economic, and Political Constraints,'' in Erhard Joeres and Martin David (eds.), *Buying a Better Environment* (Madison, Wis.: University of Wisconsin Press, 1983), pp. 1–5.

59. The Congressional Budget Office has recently analyzed these savings for the case of sulfur dioxide emissions from coal-fired electric power plants. It found that in this one case alone, annual savings would amount to $3.4 billion by the year 2000. See U.S. Congressional Budget Office, ''The Clean Air Act, the Electric Utilities, and the Coal Market'' (April 1982).

60. U.S. Environmental Protection Agency, *National Air Pollutant Emissions Estimates, 1970–1978*, Report No. EPA-450/4-80-002 (January 1980), p. 2; U.S. Environmental Protection Agency, *National Air Pollutant Emission Estimates, 1970-1981*, Report No. EPA-450/4-82-012 (September 1982), p. 2.

(except for ozone). If the research base required for setting hazardous pollutant or ambient air quality standards does not exist, the EPA should begin to fund the required research.

In water pollution policy, the EPA should begin to deal with the problem of pollution runoff from nonpoint sources (e.g., parking lots, farms, fields); it is time to address the regulatory disparity between these and other sources (industrial and sewage-treatment facilities, for example). In addition, an effort should be made to return to an approach to water-quality management that incorporates marketable discharge permits or some other form of economic incentive. This system might be controlled by the states.

In hazardous waste policy, the EPA must regain public confidence in its efforts to clean up abandoned dumpsites while looking for more sensible approaches to the general problem. Extended negotiations should be replaced by more rapid, direct action as responsible parties are given a choice of voluntary participation or litigation. At the same time, the EPA should begin to reassess the prospects for hazardous-waste management under the Resource Conservation and Recovery Act—a statute so ambitious that it cannot possibly work. Establishing new forms of strict liability or returning much of the program to state and local governments appears to be more sensible than managing millions of tons of waste in thousands of sites from Washington.

Finally, some attention must be given to simplifying environmental policy and to reducing the complexity and scope of the EPA's responsibilities. There are far too many detailed regulatory responsibilities in the major statutes that the EPA implements. The policies required by the Clean Air Act, the Resource Conservation and Recovery Act, the Toxic Substances Control Act, and the Superfund, if administered effectively and efficiently, contain the seeds of a national planning agency; but the past ten years do not offer much hope for such an ambitious, complex set of policies. Once the tumult and controversy subsides, the new EPA leadership should advance proposals for simplifying some policies and returning some tasks to the states. Nothing could be more damaging in the long run than the perception that federal environmental policy simply cannot work. The focus should be on policies that can and do work, not on those that are so ambitious or of so little value that they discredit all environmental policy.

ENERGY POLICY

William W. Hogan

After seven years with two energy crises, eight energy czars, and at least as many energy plans, the nation was ready in 1980 for President Reagan's promise of more energy production from less government involvement in energy markets. Government was said to be the cause of energy crises, not the cure. In the promised new era, reduced government regulation, curtailed energy subsidies, and sensible environmental policies would free powerful market forces to restore the United States to energy health. The few remaining energy bureaucrats would concentrate on the traditional government tasks of research and data collection. The U.S. Department of Energy would disappear.

Reagan's promises were set against a background of criticism of government initiatives that had grown steadily since the oil embargo of 1973. With oil prices higher than ever before, the policies tried or in place by 1980 had little broad-based support in the electorate and faced active opposition from the energy industry. The free-market approach offered a coherent alternative to the activist energy policy of the 1970s. Reagan administration officials presented the market as the preferred replacement for a vast array of energy programs. President Reagan and his Secretary

The work presented here reflects the careful reading and criticism of earlier drafts by Joel Darmstadter, John Deutch, Henry Lee, Paul Portney, and Daniel Yergin. The author thanks each but retains responsibility for the remaining errors, omissions, and judgments. This paper does not necessarily represent the views of these individuals or of the Energy and Environmental Policy Center, John F. Kennedy School of Government, Harvard University.

of Energy, James Edwards, set out to remove energy policy from the government agenda.[1]

The early results could hardly have been better. Almost immediately, oil prices began a steady decline. The international press was filled with stories of production cutbacks and intramural bickering among foreign oil producers. Speculation about the possible end of the energy crisis gave way to an indifferent silence. Staff members left the Department of Energy, and oil companies began to map marketing campaigns and price wars. The consumer crisis of shortage had become the industry crisis of oversupply, especially in oil and natural gas. However, there was at least one strong similarity between the actions of the Reagan administration and the much-denounced policies of Nixon, Ford, and Carter. While the free market philosophy was praised without dissent, it was practiced only within the confines of pragmatic politics. At the end of Reagan's first two years, there was more domestic reliance on government than met the eye, and too little use of the powers of government to solve the international problems of energy and security.

Oil Gluts and Gas Bubbles

On January 28, 1981, barely a week into his presidency, Ronald Reagan fulfilled his campaign promise to remove the vestiges of oil price controls established in the Nixon administration. Elimination of the controls restored an essential ingredient for workable competition in the domestic oil market. After a decade of government suppression, domestic oil prices jumped to parity with the price of imported oil. Soon, however, the nation and the world saw a glut of oil supplies and signs of cracks in the power of foreign oil producers. Within weeks oil prices began to fall. The Reagan administration offered the case of oil as an example of successful supply-side economics.

Consider the contrast with natural gas. On February 28, 1983, after two years without fulfilling his campaign promise to deregulate natural gas prices, President Reagan quietly offered the Natural Gas Consumer Regulatory Reform Amendments of 1983 to modify provisions of the Natural Gas Policy Act of 1978. Newly appointed Secretary of Energy Donald Hodel (who replaced Secretary Edwards) had fashioned a complex measure that proposed

---

1. In a review of the early days of the Reagan administration, in the *National Journal*, Richard Corrigan (p. 1280, August 18, 1981) characterized the essence of the Reagan energy policy as ". . . Duck, Defer and Deliberate. Unlike Presidents Nixon, Ford, and Carter, Ronald Reagan doesn't see energy as an urgent problem needing federal action. Instead, he puts his faith in the free market."

to change the structure of price controls on natural gas and to abrogate private contracts. Through a combination of circumstances, the market had produced a surplus of available natural gas, known as the gas "bubble," but prices were rising. The administration attributed this anomaly to the old Carter regulations, and promised a cure through new Reagan regulations. The natural gas story is an example of the Reagan administration in pursuit of a pragmatic regulatory policy.

The contrast between the Reagan oil and gas policies illustrates the debate engendered by the administration's approach to energy policy. Motivated by the general ideology of free markets, the administration entered office espousing a philosophy of limited government involvement in energy affairs. After removing the burden of government regulation, the few remaining functions of the Department of Energy were to have been dispersed to other agencies. But after two years in office, President Reagan had appointed his second secretary of energy and had been drawn into the morass of energy regulation. The substance of energy issues and the politics of energy interests had not followed his script.

Consensus on Oil

During the 1960s, gradual changes in oil markets shifted the balance of power. The Persian Gulf replaced Texas as the discretionary source of oil supply for the United States. Foreign governments were ready to replace the international oil companies in setting the prices and production levels of the crude oil extracted from their countries. In retrospect, Occidental Petroleum's 1970 decision to accept aggressive Libyan terms for its oil concession signalled the change that would have such profound effects in the decade ahead.[2]

The Arab-Israeli War of 1973 triggered the first dramatic increases in oil prices. After a small drop in production and a large rise in confusion, an oil market panic caused a sharp increase in the spot market price for crude oil. Seizing the opportunity, oil-exporting countries announced increases in the contract price of crude oil. The oil companies, with less ability to respond and a conflict of interest in higher oil prices, accepted the announcements. The governments of oil-importing countries, distracted by more pressing matters, accepted the announcements. And oil consumers, with few immediate alternatives to imported oil, accepted the announcements and paid the higher

---

2. A good discussion of the Occidental Petroleum decision to cooperate with the Libyan demands for higher prices can be found in R. Stobaugh and D. Yergin, eds., *Energy Future: Report of the Energy Project at the Harvard Business School*, (New York: Random House, 1979).

prices. During the year surrounding this first oil crisis, Persian Gulf prices rose from $2 per barrel (bbl) to more than $11 per bbl.[3]

In the United States, where domestic oil production supplied more than half of total consumption, the government could keep the average price at the pump from rising to the levels dictated by the international market by limiting the price that could be charged for domestically produced oil. The mechanism for such a limit was already in place when the oil shock occurred. Domestic oil price controls were part of the comprehensive wage and price controls established by President Nixon in August 1971. Congress quickly extended these controls and patched together a companion system of oil allocation in the Emergency Petroleum Allocation Act of 1973. Anticipating a short life for their handiwork, the oil experts from the Cost of Living Council (now moved to the Federal Energy Office) created a complex set of regulations designed to equalize oil prices across the nation and share burdens associated with the shortages.

Unfortunately, this regulatory structure created even greater shortages by suppressing prices and attempting the impossible task of managing oil logistics centrally. Gasoline lines—and political pressure—appeared; long-term solutions involving development of alternative energy supplies were actively discussed. Short-term oil policy, however, centered on the management of domestic price controls. In a close political call, President Ford signed the Energy Policy and Conservation Act of 1975, which extended price controls; in exchange, Congress agreed to create the Strategic Petroleum Reserve and establish mandatory fuel efficiency standards for automobiles. Oil price regulations grew even more complex through the creation of different categories of oil ("new" and "old," for example), each with its own regulated price. And the infamous entitlements program, which spread access to the low-cost domestic supply among all oil companies, became widely recognized as a subsidy for oil imports and a hidden source of largess for favored interest groups.

Some recognized oil price controls as counter to the best interests of the nation (artificial limits on prices blunt incentives both to conserve and produce). Even Department of Energy staff consistently denounced the program they were required to administer. It fell to President Carter to launch the gradual decontrol of oil and so to endure political heat from consumer interests.

---

3. W.L. Liscom, *The Energy Decade, 1970–1980, A Statistical and Graphical Chronicle*, (Cambridge, Mass.: Ballinger Publishing Company, 1982), p. 389.

In early 1979, Carter issued an executive order gradually decontrolling domestic oil prices; total decontrol was to be achieved in September 1981.[4]

With a second oil shock from the Iranian revolution of 1979, spot prices rose to heights that frightened even a few oil exporters. Gasoline lines reappeared and the inefficiencies of the price controls and allocation mechanisms finally became apparent to all. With domestic prices limited to half the international level, the subsidy to oil imports became an open scandal. Gradual decontrol proceeded apace; by January 1981 the average domestic price was over $32 per bbl, only $4 below its apparent market level. By the time Reagan took office, oil decontrol was no longer controversial, and he needed no new legislation to accelerate final decontrol by a few months.

It was a perfect issue for the new president. There were stark examples and shelves of studies pointing to the evils of the oil price controls. His principal constituency in the energy community wanted a symbolic refutation of past policies. The high political bill had been paid by his predecessor. There would be only minimal effects on the oil market. And President Reagan had the authority to act.

Domestic oil prices peaked in March 1981; by the end of the year refiners were paying less for their oil than they had in January (see fig. 1). The number of rotary rigs in operation and wells drilled rose 40 percent. Daily imports dropped by a million barrels,[5] and oil exporters started to organize emergency sessions to manage the oil glut. The Reagan administration confined its oil policy to claiming credit for these impressive achievements. Little mention was made of the role of President Carter, the delayed effects of the two oil price shocks, or the decline in demand from a deepening recession. It was a different matter with natural gas.

Conflict Over Gas

Found in the same regions and used for many of the same purposes, oil and natural gas are remarkably different commodities in the hands of regulators. The Natural Gas Act of 1938 established the basis for federal regulation, and the *Phillips* decision of 1954 extended controls to the wellhead price of

---

4. On April 5, 1979, President Carter made a nationally televised speech announcing his decision to decontrol domestic crude oil prices gradually (starting on June 1, 1979 and ending on October 1, 1981). At the same time he called for the windfall profits tax. See page 1 of the *New York Times*, "Carter to End Price Control on U.S. Oil and Urge Congress to Tax any 'Windfall Profits,'" Martin Tolskin and Steven Rattner (p. 1, April 6, 1979). The Windfall Profits Tax Act (P.L. 96-223, 94 Stat. 229), passed in 1980, established an excise tax on domestic crude oil.

5. U.S. Department of Energy, *Monthly Energy Review* (October 1982).

FIGURE 1

REFINER ACQUISITION COST

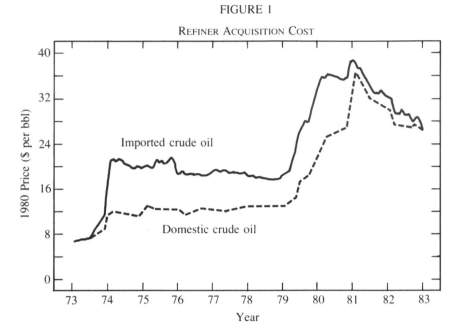

SOURCE: U.S. Department of Energy, Monthly Energy Review.

gas destined for interstate markets.[6] Regulation has been the normal condition for the natural gas industry, which grew up around its peculiar structure. By 1970, price controls had created two separate markets for natural gas. The interstate market, controlled by the federal government, was characterized by low prices, high demand, and chronic shortages; the intrastate market, free of federal regulation, experienced high and rising prices, but no excess demand. By January 1975, prices in the intrastate market were twice those of the interstate market, and the new gas supplies followed these perverse incentives. Once price controls took over, new gas flowed to the intrastate market (see fig. 2).

Because natural gas is a substitute for oil in some uses, the dramatic changes in oil prices affected the market for gas. Demand for natural gas

---

6. The Natural Gas Act of 1938 (P.L. 75-688, 52 Stat. 821) established a federal responsibility to regulate interstate natural gas sales. In the *Phillips Petroleum Co.* v. *Wisconsin* (347 U.S. 672) decision of 1954, the Supreme Court interpreted this responsibility as requiring regulation of the wellhead price of natural gas destined for the interstate market. From this decision flowed the dual market of the 1970s.

FIGURE 2

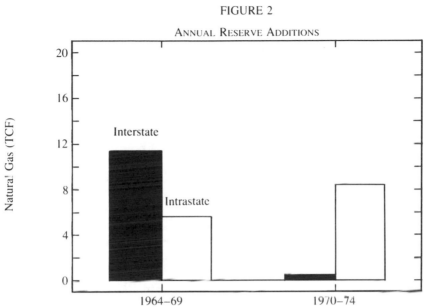

ANNUAL RESERVE ADDITIONS

SOURCE: National Energy Outlook, 1976 FEA.

rose, but supply did not, at least in the interstate market. With a cold winter in 1976 1977, deep curtailments in the supply of natural gas for industrial markets were necessary to protect residential consumers. The specter of growing natural gas shortages dominated policy development in the Carter administration, which set out to rationalize the gas market.[7]

Unlike oil markets, natural gas markets are essentially domestic. Imports amount to only 5 percent of consumption. When prices are low, demand is high and production is low, but natural gas imports cannot meet the swings. As with oil, natural gas price controls create subsidies and wealth transfers. But the major beneficiaries of oil subsidies are outside the U.S. borders and have less voice in the political debate. In the case of natural gas, however, the principal actors are well organized and have standing in the political process. The subsidy of imports from the oil entitlements program became a scandal; the consumer subsidy from natural gas price regulation became an issue for political resolution.

---

7. See the *Monthly Energy Review* (July 1976) for data on the natural gas supply and demand situation.

President Carter and his first energy czar, Secretary of Energy James Schlesinger, embarked on a lengthy legislative battle that mobilized the armies of interested producers, consumers, states, and pipeline and distribution companies. The exhausted Congress, torn by regional interests and competing loyalties, resorted to ideological standards to choose sides.[8] The result included both an intricate treaty in the form of the Natural Gas Policy Act of 1978 (NGPA), and a strong conviction on the part of the principals that this was a fight to avoid in the future.

The NGPA is an object lesson in complexity in economic regulation. Billed as an attempt to remove the burdens of regulation, the NGPA in fact extended the reach of federal regulation to the intrastate market. The act contained a bewildering array of more than twenty price categories and tiers intended to elicit the maximum production at the minimum price. Because of the need for deregulation, the NGPA incorporated a gradual schedule that would release most gas from price controls by 1985; but it also established in law the price ceilings that would apply to the gradual decontrol process.

The best defense of the NGPA was that, given the politics of the time, it was a good idea with a carefully balanced program for eventual deregulation of wellhead prices. The outcome, however, was a regulatory nightmare. The act underestimated the impact of the temporary gas shortage on the outcome of pipeline contract negotiations. Fearful of further curtailments, the natural gas pipeline companies wanted secure supplies of natural gas at any price. With a cushion of low-cost gas protected by regulation, they bid the prices of uncontrolled gas far above market levels and agreed to contracts even for supplies that might not be needed ("take-or-pay") or that guaranteed a supplier the highest price paid anyone ("most-favored-nation"). These contracts, if honored, meant an increase in consumer costs. And each twist in the regulation created a new interest group with its own positions on the NGPA.

The fatal flaw in the Natural Gas Policy Act was the attempt to legislate price ceilings. Congress set the price caps to be consistent with its forecast of world oil prices; at the time, oil prices had been stable for three years. However, no sooner had the ink dried on the new law than the oil market turmoil accompanying the Iranian revolution of 1979 upset the foundations of the act. In 1978, when the NGPA was written, imported oil was selling for $14 per bbl; two years later, when the Reagan administration entered office, imported oil cost $38 per bbl.[9] As a measure of the political problem,

---

8. For a discussion of the role of ideology, see E. Mitchell, "The Bias of Congressional Energy Policy," *Texas Law Review*, vol. 57 (March 1979), pp. 591–613.

9. See the *Monthly Energy Review* (various issues, including October 1982) for monthly reports on crude oil volumes and prices.

consider that the NGPA debate had been over a gap of only $0.69 per million British thermal units (mmBtu) between the nominal price of natural gas and the energy-equivalent price of its most important substitute, residual oil.[10] By the time President Reagan entered office, the NGPA had allowed natural gas prices to rise by more than the original gap, but with the increase in oil prices the gap had expanded by a factor of four to $2.95 per mmBtu. This presented a sizable political problem, even after taking account of the effects of inflation (see fig. 3).

This was an issue for Reagan to avoid. Every day natural gas prices rose, and every realistic option promised further increases. Interest groups were sharply divided on the issue of natural gas price decontrol. And a new political battle promised to be long and costly; President Reagan had no authority to act—new legislation would be required.

FIGURE 3

UTILITY FUEL COSTS

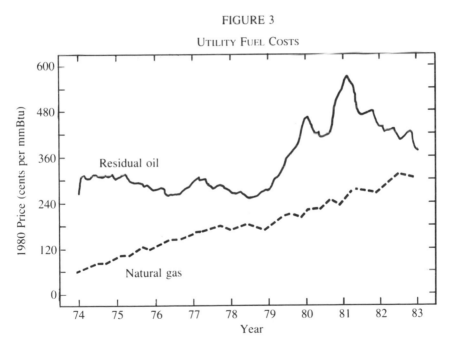

SOURCE: Department of Energy, Monthly Energy Review.

---

10. Data on the Cost of Fossil Fuels Delivered to Steam-Electric Utility Plants were taken from the *Monthly Energy Review* (April 1983), p. 92. Monthly data for earlier years were obtained from similar tables in earlier issues, including revisions.

The administration saw the wisdom of waiting for the NGPA to run its course; and through the combined effects of conservation, economic recession, warmer weather, abundant hydropower, and increased supply, a gas "bubble"—or excess supply—developed. By the end of 1982, natural gas pipeline companies were trying to reduce their purchases. But gas prices continued to rise under the formula of the NGPA. Rumors of cheap gas abounded while pipeline companies honored contracts for expensive gas. The pressure for action grew.

At the same time, oil prices were falling; change in world oil markets and the effect of the NGPA had restored the balance between oil and natural gas prices paid by the consumer.[11] There were still problems in the distribution of gas prices across individual producer contracts, but the average prices of natural gas and residual oil were nearly equal at the end of 1982. By then it was possible to argue that full decontrol of prices would have no significant effect on the prices consumers paid. It was time to act.

The administration proposal of February 28, 1983 was a masterpiece of design cut from the same cloth as the NGPA. The key ingredient was a new set of regulations leading to complete removal of controls by 1985, instead of the partial deregulation promised by the NGPA;[12] in exchange, the proposal would void the take-or-pay contracts for high-cost gas that frightened consumer interests. A curious blend of regulatory gymnastics and government intervention in private contracts, the Reagan proposal was ideologically impure. But it offered a realistic compromise for eventual movement to an unregulated market for natural gas, and it only ratified what was already under way. Faced with declining demand, pipeline companies were forcing producers to renegotiate their high-cost gas contracts and slow down wellhead deliveries.[13] The chief impact of the new regulations would be to allocate the profits among producers. With a significant fraction of natural gas production free of effective controls, the market now determined average prices paid by consumers.

---

11. A. Tussing and C. Barlow, "The Decline and Fall of Regulations," *Energy Journal*, vol. 3, no. 4 (October 1982), pp. 103–122.

12. Secretary Hodel announced the Reagan natural gas deregulation proposal on February 28, 1983. The U.S. General Accounting Office produced a detailed "Analysis of the Administration Natural Gas Decontrol Plan," on April 11, 1983.

13. On September 17, 1982, the *New York Times* reported that "Gas is Plentiful but Prices Are Up." But one year later, on September 16, 1983, the *Wall Street Journal* reported on the effects of a major pipeline company, Transco, to restructure its contracts and lower the cost of gas.

Victory Declared

The contrast between the oil and gas policies of the Reagan administration reveals a consistent dedication to free-market principles and an equally consistent attention to political pragmatism and compromise. The administration, like many experts, argues that insulating consumers from market prices only causes greater harm in the long term; furthermore, the government has no business interfering with business. But this philosophy has not caused the administration to take actions that would incur great political costs, such as decontrol of natural gas in 1981. Nor has it prevented government interference with business in an attempt to achieve longer-term goals.

From this perspective, the Reagan oil and gas policy can be seen as a pragmatic and linear extension of the Carter policy. The dominant factor was change in world oil markets. The delayed effects of the first two oil shocks contributed to the economic recession and the acceleration of energy conservation. With the resulting decline in the demand for energy, the price of the marginal source, imported oil, began to fall. At the start of the Reagan administration, oil price controls were nearly gone and world oil prices were likely to fall further; not so for natural gas. A smart politician would decontrol oil and avoid the gas problem. Two years later, the price controls on gas had become largely ineffective, gas prices were likely to follow oil prices; it was possible to declare victory again. The realistic observer can find merit in this approach. But evaluations of Reagan's oil and gas policies must take into account the importance of the larger events and the difficult decisions made in the previous administration.

Energy and Security

The free-market principles of Reagan's energy policy, which have a compelling logic, find adequate empirical support in the case of the domestic oil market. Deviations from workable competition among domestic oil producers and marketers appear small or amenable to remedies less drastic than federal price controls over each well. Given the established price of imported oil, there is little that individual companies can do to affect market outcomes on the scale of price changes in the 1970s. However, reliance on the free market does not travel well in the international oil market, which sets the price of imported oil, or when applied to the problems of energy and security. The risks of universally applying free market theories become apparent in treating the problems of international oil.

The international oil market, dominated by a few producers, does not remotely approximate the free market that is thought to have such attractive efficiencies. The difficulties that governments in oil-producing countries face in disciplining the market or in extracting the exorbitant profits to which they aspire should not be confused with competitive market conditions in which prices are close to long-term marginal costs. For example, in 1983 Saudi Arabia agreed to a 13 percent price reduction, the first such reduction after a cumulative 1,200 percent increase over the preceding decade; however, Saudi Arabia was producing at only 50 percent of capacity. This is hardly evidence of a competitive market in the conventional sense. The forces of supply and demand play a role that the producers cannot ignore, but it is self-deceptive for the administration or others to argue that these forces dominate the market or function in the best interests of the United States.[14]

The domestic energy debate of the 1970s focused largely on the issue of who should pay the increased oil bill. The Reagan administration is on firm ground when it argues that the government should let the market decide this question, which is at heart a value judgment, a political choice that the 1980 election delegated to the administration. Both producers and consumers can claim the profits, but the government need not show preference for one group over the other. The government should be interested only in promoting the efficiency gains that flow from market pricing of oil.

But this logic is turned on its head in the international market. Here there is a strong case to be made for a government interest in maximizing the opportunity for the United States to capture the economic benefit. The oil exporters restrict production and reduce world welfare while increasing their own income. The United States could intervene in the world market to re-capture a portion of this value. Although the government may take the position that it has no preferences in the allocation of wealth among U.S. citizens, the government should be highly interested in the allocation of wealth between its citizens and those of other countries.

Oil security provides a second anchor for government policy. Catastrophes in the oil market will raise costs and curtail supplies for all consumers. Yet individual consumers cannot adjust their market decisions to accommodate all the costs of a major oil emergency. The vulnerability of oil supplies provides another traditional argument for government involvement in energy

---

14. The absence of a free market is further revealed by the comparison of marginal costs and prices. The cost of production in Saudi Arabia is under $1 per barrel, compared to $10 and up in frontier areas. Yet it is not the high-cost oil that faces an uncertain market. The high-priced oil from Saudi Arabia absorbs the production swings needed to maintain the high world oil price.

markets. Major interruptions in world oil markets are quite possible in the next decade; these disruptions can translate into macroeconomic catastrophes. (Much worse—armed conflict—is also possible. The threat to oil security was used, for example, to justify creation of the Rapid Deployment Force.)[15] The higher inflation, increased unemployment, and greater transfer of wealth that result from oil supply interruptions are real economic costs that are not recognized in individual market transactions. This market failure implies that the imported oil price does not provide the correct signal to domestic markets.[16]

Government intervention in energy and security problems could take many forms. In the first two years of the Reagan administration, the principal government efforts were the Strategic Petroleum Reserve and emergency preparedness programs.

The Strategic Petroleum Reserve

A sudden disparity between supply and demand can be relieved by a stockpile that can be rushed to the market. This is the logic behind the Strategic Petroleum Reserve (SPR). The importance of oil and the extent of the externalities surrounding its consumption dictate a stockpile size well beyond reasonable expectations for private inventories. In a succession of studies in and out of government, various authors concluded that the optimal size for the United States stockpile was in excess of one billion barrels.[17] Without controversy, the Energy Policy and Conservation Act of 1975 established the SPR program authorizing a reserve of one billion barrels and establishing an interim goal of 500 million barrels in place by 1980.

The agreement on goals did not translate into agreement on implementation, however. The optimal time for stockpile purchases always seemed to be "later;" by 1980 the SPR amounted to only 91 million barrels, and new purchases had been suspended. A frustrated Congress directed in a provision of the Energy Security Act of 1980 that purchases should be at least 100,000

---

15. The Rapid Development Force is frequently described as meeting the need to defend Persian Gulf Oil, for example, see W. Beeman, "Sharing Defense of the Gulf," *New York Times* (February 9, 1983, p. 29).

16. For a further discussion of market failures and the question of oil vulnerability, see D. Deese and J. Nye, eds., *Energy and Security* (Cambridge, Mass.: Ballinger Publishing Co., 1981). The arguments apply to trade in any commodity. The usual reason for avoiding interference in free trade is limited leverage from commodities that make up a small part of the economy and the danger of retaliation. Neither argument applies to oil, which enjoys a large value share in the United States economy, is the major commodity involved in international trade, and is already subject to restrictive practices on the part of the oil exporters.

17. For a review of the estimates of the optimal stockpile size, see W. Hogan, "Oil Stockpiling: Help Thy Neighbor," *Energy Journal*, vol. 4, no. 3 (July 1983).

bbl a day. Constrained by this law, the Reagan administration has a better performance record than its predecessor. By 1982 the SPR had reached nearly 300 million barrels, and it stood at 360 million barrels by the end of 1983. However, the administration did as little as possible, and has continued to argue the free-market case against the SPR. Congress responded in the Energy Emergency Preparedness Act of 1982 by increasing the minimum fill rate to 220,000 bbl a day.[18] The new targets are 500 million barrels by 1985 and 750 million barrels by 1989. The Government Accounting Office (GAO) reports that storage capacity limits threaten this schedule.[19]

Administration animus toward the SPR is manifest in its policy on planning for emergencies and the use of the oil stockpile. Experience with other strategic stockpiles suggests that efficient use of the reserve in an emergency cannot be taken for granted.[20] Bureaucrats familiar with the issue have struggled to make the case for prudent preparation for use of the SPR, but the administration has actively avoided such preparations. When Congress required a plan, the administration complied with the form but not the substance of the law. In its review of the "Strategic Petroleum Reserve Drawdown Plan," the GAO concluded: "In summary, we found that the SPR Plan and Report give little specific information on how the SPR could be used in an oil supply disruption . . . . the administration's arguments against such planning are unconvincing."[21] The message from the White House is clear: energy problems can be solved better by markets than by governments. This view appears again in the approach to planning other elements of emergency preparedness.

Emergency Preparedness

Convinced that less government preparation now guarantees less government involvement later, the Reagan administration has complied with the letter of emergency preparedness laws but has endorsed the free market approach to the management of oil emergencies. Oil consumers will be free to

---

18. The law mandates a minimum fill of 300,000 bbl per day unless the president finds it not in the national interest, in which case the minimum fill rate must be 220,000 bbl per day. The president so determined for 1983.

19. U.S. Government Accounting Office, *The United States Remains Unprepared for Oil Import Disruptions* (Washington, D.C.: September 1981).

20. Under conventional wisdom, at the start of an emergency the fear of a worsening situation leads to an unwillingness to use the reserves. Hence the stockpile is preserved until the last instead of being used at the beginning to stem panic.

21. Reported in a letter to Senators James McClure and Bennett Johnson from J.D. Pearch, director, U.S. General Accounting Office, "Status of Strategic Petroleum Reserve Activities as of December 31, 1982," GAO/RCED-83-93, (January 14, 1983), p. 6.

bid up the price of oil during interruptions and make the oil exporters the beneficiaries of oil emergencies.

No amount of preparation can hope to eliminate fully the costs of oil disruptions, but steps could be taken to minimize damages. For example, a domestic tax and a scheme for early dispersal of funds ("prebates") to re-distribute the economic loss could be put in place in advance.[22] If this plan handled the bulk of the distributional and consumer equity complaints, it might be possible to leave domestic markets free to allocate the scarce oil supplies. Otherwise, political pressure to reimpose oil price controls would probably be overwhelming.

The International Energy Agency (IEA) also awaits a U.S. initiative to create an added tool for meeting oil emergencies.[23] Established by a treaty among oil importers, the IEA began in 1974 with the goal of fashioning a coordinated program for managing energy emergencies. This has proved to be an elusive goal. The IEA is now no more than an information-sharing vehicle; and valuable as this service may be, it provides far less help than the IEA's intended purpose—to serve as a mechanism for balancing oil sup-plies in an emergency and stopping precipitous increases in spot oil prices. Other actions of the Reagan administration have also reduced the likelihood of coordinated international action to reduce the damage of oil market dis-ruptions. The Japanese can hardly be sanguine about the prospects for co-operation with an administration that has sidestepped the removal of restrictions on the export of Alaskan oil;[24] and the Europeans can be expected to have diminished fervor for cooperation after the heavy-handed treatment they re-ceived over the Yamburg pipeline and European purchases of Soviet natural gas.[25]

---

22. A. Alm, "Energy Supply Interruptions and National Security," *Science*, vol. 211 (March 27, 1981), pp. 1379–1385.

23. The International Energy Program (IEP) is the mechanism through which the member countries of the International Energy Agency are to coordinate their responses to oil emergencies. For a critique of the IEP, see W. Hogan, "Policies for Oil Importers," in J. Griffin and D. Teece, eds., *OPEC Behavior and World Oil Prices* (London: Allen and Unwin, 1982).

24. Parallel stories in the *New York Times*, "Alaskan Oil Export Issue is Revived," Douglas Martin, (August 13, 1981, p. 25) and "Alaska Oil Export Idea is Revived," Robert D. Hershey, (February 10, 1983, p. 24) reflect the continuing rhetoric without action on this initiative to open exports to Japan.

25. For example, Prime Minister Margaret Thatcher criticized the United States for at-tempting to prevent foreign companies from fulfilling contracts to build the Yamburg pipeline, which was to bring gas from Siberia to markets in Western Europe (*New York Times*, "Mrs. Thatcher Faults U.S. on Siberian Pipeline," James Fearon, July 2, 1982, p. 1). For a further discussion of the Yamburg pipeline, see B. Greer and J. Russell, "European Reliance on Soviet Natural Gas Exports: The Yamburg-Urengoi Natural Gas Project," *Energy Journal*, vol 3, no. 3 (July 1982), pp. 15–37.

The administration's principal defense of unpreparedness rests on the glut in the oil market and the low probability of an oil supply interruption. These circumstances should be viewed as an opportunity for action, not a time for relaxation. A time when there is little pressure on world oil markets is the best time to prepare for the moment when the market grows tight and the danger arises again. Few doubt that Persian Gulf oil will continue to be of central importance in future world oil markets, or that its supply will continue to depend on the stability of an unstable region. It is reasonable to expect a resumption of tight market conditions in the late 1980s, and most real preparations take several years to put in place. The current oil glut was purchased at a high cost in inflation and recession. The opportunity it offers should not be sacrificed to the invisible hand of the free market.

A Tariff on Oil

Because of the several externalities cited above, the free market does not provide the level of oil imports that is in the best interest of oil-importing nations. Only the government can intervene to affect import demand for the benefit of the nation. The most direct method for such intervention is the imposition of an oil import tariff. The Reagan administration has not proposed such a tariff, but press reports indicate an active consideration of this option. A tariff would provide the Treasury with a much-needed source of revenue; this may be the most important factor in favor of a politically unattractive measure that would raise prices. To the extent that the tariff is lower than the economically justified level, other policies of oil demand and supply management may be needed.

The economic justification of an oil import tariff is not in doubt. A tariff in the range of 30 percent to 40 percent of the price of oil is robust across many assumptions, and this is surely at the upper end of the politically feasible.[26] There are many alternative forms for an oil tariff; for example, the president could impose a fee on each barrel of imported oil under current law, and Congress would have to take action to stop implementation.[27] With new legislation, a tariff could be set as a fixed percentage of the price of oil

---

26. For discussions of oil tariffs, see D. Bohi and D. Montgomery, *Oil Prices, Energy Security and Import Policy* (Washington, D.C.: Resources for the Future, 1982). For an analysis of the robustness of the optimal tariff estimate, see W. Hogan, "Oil Gluts and Oil Tariffs," Discussion Paper, Energy and Environmental Policy Center, Harvard University (May 1982).

27. Presidents Eisenhower, Nixon, and Ford have used the authority of the Trade Agreement Extension Act of 1955 to impose quotas (Eisenhower) and fees (Nixon and Ford) on oil imports. The fees have stirred congressional concern. President Ford withdrew his fees as part of the negotiations over the Energy Policy and Conservation Act of 1975. In 1978, President Carter

imports; such an *ad valorem* tariff would adjust automatically to market conditions.

A percentage tariff would protect U.S. consumers from the consequences of uncertain judgment about world oil prices. The dangers of legislating fixed prices based on exact forecasts of market trends were illustrated all too clearly by the NGPA. Furthermore, a proportional tariff would make it easier to accommodate differences in the quality of crude oils. And the same tariff applied to product imports should minimize distortions of choices across petroleum products.

A tariff could also produce a great deal of money for the federal government. The effects would be complex. On balance, however, the Congressional Budget Office estimated that selected tariffs would produce the revenues shown in table 1.[28]

Such revenues could help reduce the federal deficit and offer the attendant benefits of lower interest rates and accelerated economic recovery. There is another source of institutional failure that an import tariff may be able to help correct. An oil import tariff is one of the few large-scale taxes that helps more than it hurts. If the administration can overcome its objection to taxes per se, this source of revenue and improved operation of energy markets should be seized while the fleeting opportunity remains for an easy transition in a glut market.

TABLE 1

OIL IMPORT TARIFF REVENUES
(Billions of Dollars)

Tariff	Fiscal Year				
	1983	*1984*	*1985*	*1986*	*1987*
$2/bbl	4.7	4.2	4.2	5.3	4.9
$5/bbl	9.8	9.4	10.5	13.2	12.4
$10/bbl	21.4	19.8	19.1	24.4	21.9

SOURCE: CBO [1982], adjusted for changes in net outlays relative to $5 tariff.
NOTE: The budgetary effects are for the case when the world price drops by one-third of the tariff. If prices do not drop, the U.S. government collects more revenue, but so do the oil exporters, and the United States gains less from the tariff.

---

threatened to impose a $5 per barrel fee and narrowly defeated a Congressional vote to remove his authority to impose a fee. Later President Carter promised to consult with Congress before imposing any fee. For a further discussion, see *Congressional Quarterly Almanac*, vol. 31 (1975), p. 196, and vol. 34 (1978), p. 104.

28. Congressional Budget Office, "Oil Import Tariffs: Alternative Scenarios and Their Effects," Staff Working Paper (Washington, D.C.: April 1982).

The principal political objection to an oil import tariff is that it would reduce the competitiveness of energy-intensive exports. The simple response is that the United States should be eager to reduce the sales of goods that are priced below cost. However, the complaint will not be dismissed easily, and the political power of the exporters may be great enough to require special subsidies.

The most serious economic objection to an oil import tariff is the threat that intervention in any market poses to the larger fabric of international trade. However, the oil cartel—or at least its leading members—has already abandoned any pretense that oil price and production follow a free market in international trade. Artificial restrictions on oil production have reduced total world economic output while greatly enriching the few oil exporters. Intervention by the oil importers could be viewed as redressing the balance, not as upsetting the international applecart.

In terms of the effect on their oil markets, the United States' major trading partners, as fellow oil importers, should view a reduction of U.S. oil demand as in their own interest. Certainly calls for U.S. oil conservation have consistently come from the International Energy Agency. However, a tariff on oil might become a precedent or excuse for restrictions on the trade of other goods; the United States might look to less ideologically offensive and more indirect methods for restricting oil imports. This would be one justification for an expansion of the modest 5-cents-per-gallon gasoline tax passed by the 97th Congress. Other importers should not object if the United States adopts domestic oil taxes of a magnitude similar to those found in Europe and Japan. In short, legitimate concern over the protection of the international trading system might modify the type of import restriction but need not cause the United States to forego the value of reducing oil imports.

Energy Production and Conservation

All forms of energy are affected by changes in the international oil market. The need to shift away from expensive and vulnerable oil supplies causes more energy to be produced and conserved. The principal policy choices are in the degree and type of government involvement, the relative emphasis on production and conservation, and the selection of favored energy forms. The clear preferences of the Reagan administration are revealed through individual actions and budget proposals: less government involvement, production rather than conservation, and the promotion of nuclear power.

Budget Proposals

The Reagan vision of a sharply reduced role for government stands out in a comparison of the expenditures anticipated by President Carter in his last budget and the corresponding energy outlays planned by President Reagan in his first full budget message (see fig. 4).[29] The major Carter initiative was

TABLE A
CARTER'S BUDGETED ENERGY OUTLAYS
(Fiscal Year 1982 Submission)

Supply	(Billions of 1980 Dollars)				
	FY80	*FY81*	*FY82[a]*	*FY83[a]*	*FY84[a]*
Solar	0.53	0.53	0.47	0.48	0.45
Fossil	0.82	0.88	1.15	1.20	1.12
Fission	1.14	0.82	1.05	0.91	0.92
Other R&D	1.29	1.29	1.51	1.23	1.26
Total R&D	3.78	3.52	4.18	3.82	3.75
Other supply	0.79	1.33	0.81	0.66	0.48
Total supply	4.57	4.85	4.99	4.45	4.23
Conservation	0.57	0.68	0.85	0.80	0.64
Emergency preparedness	0.34	2.97	2.73	2.98	1.85
EIA, policy, regulation	0.88	0.85	1.05	0.94	0.92
Total energy	6.36	9.35	9.62	9.20	7.64

a. Figures for 1983 through 1984 are projected outlays from submission of FY1982.

TABLE B
REAGAN'S BUDGETED ENERGY OUTLAYS
(Fiscal Year 1983 Submission)

Supply	(Billions of 1980 Dollars)					
	FY80	*FY81*	*FY82*	*FY83[a]*	*FY84[a]*	*FY85[a]*
Solar	0.53	0.53	0.38	0.12	0.06	0.06
Fossil	0.82	0.88	0.55	0.16	0.21	0.20
Fission	1.14	0.82	1.00	0.67	0.63	0.60
Other R&D	1.29	1.29	0.83	0.82	0.70	0.72
Total R&D	3.78	3.52	2.76	1.77	1.60	1.58
Other supply	0.79	1.33	−0.12	0.56	0.35	0.36
Total supply	4.57	4.85	2.64	2.33	1.95	1.94
Conservation	0.57	0.68	0.43	0.26	0.12	0.01
Emergency preparedness	0.34	2.97	1.64	2.42	2.00	1.85
EIA, policy, regulation	0.88	0.85	0.74	0.54	0.54	0.48
Total energy	6.36	9.35	5.45	5.55	4.61	4.28

NOTE: Totals may not add owing to small offsetting receipts and independent rounding.
a. Figures for 1983 through 1985 are projected outlays from the budget submission of FY 1983.

29. The data on the budget appear in the fiscal year 1982 budget submission of President Carter and the fiscal year 1983 budget submission of President Reagan. The following tables summarize the principal categories.

FIGURE 4

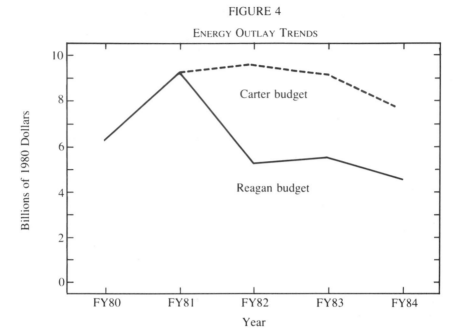

ENERGY OUTLAY TRENDS

SOURCE: Federal budgets FY 82 and FY 83.

to complete the by-then-overdue oil stockpile. Aside from the temporary increases to fill the SPR, the Carter plan called for about constant real expenditures on energy. On the same basis, the Reagan plan called for a 60 percent reduction in outlays. The full Reagan reductions did not survive congressional review, but the comparison reveals the speed at which previous energy policies are being reversed.

Quoted as believing that energy conservation leaves you "too cold in the winter and too hot in the summer," President Reagan set out to abolish the federal programs of conservation research and development, state aid, and efficiency standard development. Energy conservation had come full circle since 1973: ideological outcast, conventional wisdom, ideological outcast.

When David Freeman published his low energy demand scenario in 1974 he was criticized as a dreamer;[30] but the Energy Research and Development

30. D. Freeman, *A Time to Choose*, A Preliminary Report of the Energy Policy Project of the Ford Foundation, New York (1974). The "Zero Energy Growth" scenario projected 1980 demand of 87 quadrillion Btus.

Administration, a forerunner of the Department of Energy, soon after ran into a storm of criticism for a plan that failed to acknowledge the possibility of lower energy demand through conservation.[31] President Carter wrapped himself in a symbolic sweater and made conservation the conceptual (but not budgetary) cornerstone of his energy policy. As 1980 passed it became apparent that Freeman had actually overpredicted gross demand by almost 15 percent.[32] Adjusting for the effects of economic activity, energy intensity measured as Btus per dollar of gross national product declined by a remarkable 20 percent between 1973 and 1982.[33]

The Reagan administration's antipathy to government involvement in energy conservation extends to most forms of energy supply research. The administration slashed funds for solar energy research and imposed nearly as dramatic a reduction on the fossil fuels program. The administration preference for production over conservation is largely a preference for nuclear energy over conservation and other forms of supply (see fig. 5). Nuclear fission is the largest single beneficiary of government funds, and nuclear fusion makes up a significant fraction of the remaining programs shown under "other supply." The Reagan budget looks much like the last pre-oil-embargo budget, with a heavy tilt toward nuclear power.[34]

The preference for nuclear power is curious, given the changes in the nature of the market. Aside from economic and safety problems, the nuclear industry has been noteworthy for its rapid decrease in planned capacity. In 1975 there were 236 nuclear units operational, under construction, or planned; since then there have been 92 cancellations, and more are expected. Electricity load growth is dramatically lower and there is little likelihood that nuclear power will enjoy the bright future once envisioned.

The prize of the nuclear program, the Clinch River breeder reactor, was the most egregious example of the misdirection of the nuclear subsidies. The

---

31. The first plan of the Energy Research and Development Administration, known as ERDA-48, was criticized for ignoring energy conservation. For a review of the controversy, see M. Greenberger, *Caught Unawares: The Energy Decade in Retrospect* (Cambridge, Mass.: Ballinger Publishing Co., 1983).

32. See the *Monthly Energy Review* (April 1983). Actual consumption in 1980 was 75.9 quadrillion Btus. As mentioned above, the forecast of 87 quadrillion Btus overestimated demand by 15 percent.

33. See the *Monthly Energy Review* (April 1983).

34. According to the federal budget for fiscal year 1984 (see Appendices, FY 1984 Budget Submission, table 20, applying the deflators implicit in table 23), total expenditures on energy for fiscal year 1974, the last budget set before the oil embargo, were $1.35 billion 1980 dollars compared with the Reagan proposal of $2.38 billion for fiscal year 1985, net of expenditures for the Strategic Petroleum Reserve. This compares with the Carter peak of $6.28 billion net in fiscal year 1981. The Reagan increases relative to fiscal year 1974 are concentrated in nuclear programs.

FIGURE 5

COMPARATIVE OUTLAYS, FISCAL YEAR 1984

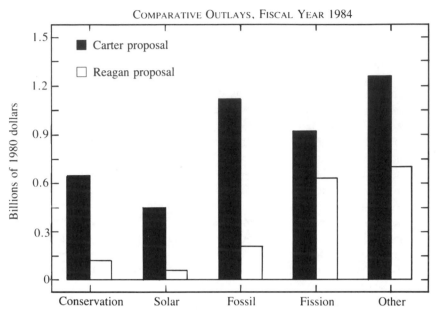

SOURCE: Federal Budgets FY 82 and FY 83

GAO reported that the plant could cost twenty times as much as the original estimate of $400 million. The Carter administration fought Clinch River as uneconomic and technologically obsolete.[35] Its supporters in the Reagan administration have not explained how the breeder program, conceived at a time when uranium was expected to be expensive and the development of nuclear power was accelerating, preserved its urgency in the face of abundant uranium supplies and a deceleration in nuclear power programs. After two years in office, the Reagan administration saw the window for the breeder moved far into the next century. But until the Senate voted to terminate the Clinch River project in the fall of 1983, the administration was backing a compromise designed to keep it alive.

On its face, the Clinch River project might be dismissed as pork-barrel politics for powerful congressional interests. But the Reagan policy was consistent with a broader theme of support for nuclear power. For example, in

---

35. For a summary of the critiques of the Clinch River Breeder project, see the *National Journal*, "Clinch River Breeder Project Draws Opposition of Strange Bedfellows," by William J. Lanquette, (October 2, 1982), pp. 1678–1679.

his October 1981 policy statement on nuclear energy, Reagan lifted Carter's ban on the reprocessing of spent nuclear fuel and boosted opportunities for international trade in plutonium.[36] It is difficult to fathom this special interest in nuclear power. The federal subsidy is inconsistent with the free-market philosophy of the administration; the market has turned away from starting any new nuclear power plants.

The internal contradictions of administration policy also reveal themselves in the arguments about synthetic fuels. After several false starts, the supporters of synthetic fuels saw President Carter sign the Energy Security Act of 1980. This law established the Synthetic Fuels Corporation (SFC), authorized as much as $88 billion for production supports over the next decade, and set a series of ambitious targets for developing synthetic fuels, with a prime focus on Colorado shale oil. Soon after the SFC came into being, the newly elected Reagan administration announced its intention to eliminate the corporation and leave the synthetic fuels business to the private sector. Pundits enjoyed the bust of the fourth federal shale oil boom since 1915.[37]

Whatever the merits of the SFC, the arguments in favor of support of nuclear power apply with equal force to synthetic fuels. The United States has abundant energy resources that want only the technology to provide direct substitutes for imported oil. There is large capital investment required, a high degree of uncertainty, and a range of environmental concerns. Yet the administration supports nuclear fuel subsidies while turning away from synthetic fuels. The contradiction may flow from the heavy ideological bent of administration policy. In the case of energy, the ideology starts with an answer: more markets, more nuclear. But this answer cannot endure close scrutiny. And ideology stands in contrast to social cost-benefit analysis as a guide to the role of government.

Government Involvement

It is not easy to determine the appropriate role of government in energy policy. The needs for safety and environmental regulation and of rules for governing private exchange are recognized as major sources of government

---

36. For a review of the debate surrounding the international trade in plutonium, see *National Journal* "Reagan Loosens Controls on Plutonium and Unleashes a Flood of Worries," William J. Lanquette (August 7, 1982), pp. 1376–1378.

37. For a thorough discussion of the history of energy policy, including epochs in synthetic fuels policy, see C. Goodwin, *Energy Policy in Perspective: Today's Problems, Yesterday's Solutions* (Washington, D.C.: Brookings Institution, 1981). For an investigation of a framework for designing a future synthetic fuels policy, see J. Harlan, *Starting with Synfuels: Benefits, Costs and Program Design Assessments* (Cambridge, Mass.: Ballinger Publishing Co., 1982).

involvement in energy activities; for example, there is little controversy over the necessity of a body such as the Nuclear Regulatory Commission to oversee the safe operation of nuclear power plants. The federal energy budget includes funding for the Federal Energy Regulatory Commission in its role as the regulator of the natural monopolies in interstate sales of gas and wholesale transactions of electric power. Although there is disagreement about the proper degree and form of such regulation, there is little argument about the proper role of government in these cases. Indeed, most of the substantive debate on the stringency of safety and environmental regulation stems from strong disagreement over the role of government in economic regulation of markets not clearly delineated as natural monopolies.

A traditional economic rationale for government involvement in a primarily private economy is to serve to correct market failures. When the market fails to align public and private interests, only the government can intervene to realign consumers' and producers' choices. The putative failures in energy markets are several; there are, for example, the externalities associated with imported oil and the resulting gap between social and private costs. Regulation of electric utilities violates the basic assumption that the market will set prices equal to marginal costs. Average cost pricing of electricity virtually guarantees a divergence between social and private costs at the margin as perceived by the ultimate consumer. (Also, conservation supporters often point to the problem of enticing renters to conserve on energy, especially in centrally metered buildings.) Information and learning curve externalities, where a successful innovation cannot be kept secret for long, may lead to private underinvestment in research and development. Capital markets are probably not perfect. And so on.

The Reagan administration counters these arguments with the valid observation that the increase in energy prices since 1973 provided ample incentive for improved energy efficiency and expanded production. This turns on its head the oft-repeated conservationist argument that improved energy efficiency is the cheapest source of supply. If it takes a long time to adjust to a sudden change of energy prices, then there must be a reservoir of untapped opportunities that do not require government support. This would explain the marked improvement in energy efficiency and the apparent surplus of energy supply.[38]

That this argument summarizes an important truth makes it more difficult to recognize its irrelevance in determining the role of government. Public intervention need not replace the market, but it should influence the choices

---

38. See in particular the comments of Danny J. Boggs, executive secretary of the Cabinet Council on Natural Resources, as reported in the *National Journal* (August 18, 1981), p. 1282.

made at the margin, where the differences between public and private costs could swing a decision. The Reagan administration instead focuses on the change induced by higher prices and confuses the difference between average and marginal effects. There are tremendous private opportunities for energy conservation and production, on the average, and these profitable opportunities should be exploited without government help. But on the margin these opportunities fall short of balancing social costs and benefits. And it is here that the case is made for government involvement in the economic decisions of the private market.

The distinction between average and marginal choices simplifies the definition of the role of government, but it complicates the design and execution of the proper government program. The challenge is to find opportunities for conservation and production that are attractive enough to be socially beneficial but unattractive enough to be forgone in the private market. It is a delicate balance that challenges government; and the story of the Synthetic Fuels Corporation is a case in point.

The Synthetic Fuels Corporation. When Congress passed the Energy Security Act of 1980, motivated by the fear of supply disruptions, it placed heavy emphasis on an early synthetic fuels program with large-scale production. This can be recognized as the wrong solution to the problem of oil supply vulnerability. New synthetic fuels production would be too little and too late, and would besides involve technologies known to be uneconomic. The high-production scheme was directed at the wrong problem. A cost/ benefit case for synthetic fuels would rest on a different argument about the failure of the oil market.

When Edward Noble was appointed chairman of the SFC in late 1981, he endorsed the administration's market policy and promised to rid the nation of the organization he had been appointed to head. Later he noticed that there was a substantial domestic energy resource base that might be exploited if a technology with acceptable economics could be found. If fuel prices suddenly rose, there would be a need for rapid acceleration of synthetic fuels production and it might pay to get a head start. And for all the reasons that apply to general government support of research and development, private investment would fall short of the appropriate level, especially given the long-term uncertainties in the world oil market.

However, the optimal program would not be an $88 billion production extravaganza concentrating on a few technologies. A better program would involve a moderate expense of $10 billion to $15 billion spent on a wide range of small projects with different technologies and targeted on different resources. This would break ground for the private market, not attempt to replace it. By early 1983, Edward Noble was characterizing the program that had evolved under his leadership as an insurance program that provided a prudent investment for the nation.[39] His next challenge is to make the case to the rest of the administration and to Congress.

The U.S. Department of Energy.   Noble was not alone in promising to disband the organization he was appointed to head; a similar action was at the top of the 1981 agenda of newly appointed Secretary of Energy James Edwards. The most visible administration promise in the energy domain, the dismantling of the Department of Energy, took on vindictive overtones; in effect, the administration painted the entire organization with the brush of one program, the oil price controls. Yet the department itself had spoken out against controls, and most of its activity was concentrated in less controversial work that would continue under any organizational structure. A GAO critique found no support for the claimed savings of reorganization.[40]

Congress did not encourage the department's reorganization, and for some time there was no decision in favor of reorganization and none against it, leading to confusion and uncertainty. The merits of the dispute are meager. The advantages of maintaining the department to provide advice and direction are subject to the willingness of the administration to listen to the advice or use the leadership. Leaving the department in place would at least give some stability to an area of government where chronic instability has been at the root of many of the annoying fumbles of the past. Fortunately, the issue is fading and will be resolved in the arena of symbolic power struggles between the White House and Capitol Hill.

Summary

Falling oil prices should be on every politician's Christmas list. The Reagan administration's wish was granted; energy markets became calmer as it took office. The energy policy of the Carter administration had little effect on the energy crisis it weathered; the Reagan administration deserves little credit for the currently relatively abundant supplies of oil and natural gas.

Reliance on the free market is a good starting point for viewing energy policy in the Reagan administration, but there is less here than meets the eye.

---

39. For example, see "Chairman Noble: From Synfuels Opponent to Advocate," *National Journal* (May 7, 1983).

40. The U.S. General Accounting Office analyzed the putative savings of the proposed reorganization of the Department of Energy and concluded that they were without foundation. See "Analysis of Energy Reorganization Savings Estimates and Plans" (EMD-82-77), August 2, 1982.

The decontrol of oil advanced by only eight months the plan launched by Carter; and when it came to the harder issue of natural gas, the administration chose to duck. Free-market principles were put on hold until the problems became less troublesome, and then the administration offered a welcome dose of pragmatism by adding to the long history of well-intentioned natural gas regulatory structures.

In the natural gas debate the administration risked using solutions that would be outmoded rapidly by changes in the market. The existing regulations arose in response to shortage. The administration alternative, designed in response to surplus, could collapse under the pressure of another shortage. But it is still possible, thanks to the administration, that the free market for natural gas production will appear before the next regulatory fix.

Evidence of a less than consistent market policy appeared in the administration's energy budget, which cuts total expenditures but expands the nuclear component. Given the nature of energy markets, the unavoidable involvements of government, and market externalities, the case for an active government role in compensating for market failures is coherent and well enough supported to deserve a better hearing from the Reagan administration. Although there is ample room for differences about the particulars of program design, the nation has not been well served by the Reagan administration slogans that have been offered as substitutes for analysis of energy policy options.

The Reagan energy policy rings most hollow on the budget balance between nuclear power and its alternatives. No matter the failings of previous conservation, solar, and fossil programs; there is no justification for abandoning these government programs in favor of nuclear technology. In addition to the imbalance in the federal energy budget, the overall level of funding is too low. It strains credulity to claim that the last federal budget developed before the oil embargo of 1973, when energy was thought to be cheap and plentiful, had nearly the right funding level for the 1980s; but this is the implication of administration policy.

Forgone opportunities are most obvious with respect to preparations for oil emergencies. The oil market is soft and the energy crisis seems to have vanished—but oil consumers paid a high price for this interlude. Declining oil prices will stimulate demand, and the hoped-for economic recovery is most eagerly awaited in the capitals of the oil exporters. The administration is letting the opportunity slip away.

The energy bill will come due again.

AGRICULTURAL POLICY

Bruce Gardner

A typical U.S. farmer today is, on the whole, in better financial health than congressional and media testimony suggest (although some commercial farmers are in serious trouble). The farmers' relative prosperity does not, however, reduce the political importance of agricultural policy. The Reagan administration has made some important innovations in agricultural policy—the 1983 payment-in-kind (PIK) program, for example, and an effort to hold price supports down. These and other actions, some more successful than others, can be best understood in the context of earlier policies and current economic conditions.

Background

Government intervention in the economics of U.S. agriculture has been accepted for many years. Two rationales support this intervention: first, that without intervention farm prices and incomes would be too low; and second, that agricultural commodity prices are too unstable. The first belief is widespread; for example, the public statements of legislators who support aid to farmers express concern that many farmers are on the verge of bankruptcy or at least receive woefully inadequate returns for their efforts. Some recent statements are as strong as those heard in the 1930s.[1]

And the press agrees. When Senator Jim Sasser (D-Tennessee) introduced his Emergency Farm Stabilization Act of 1983, he inserted in the record some

---

1. For example, Rep. Bill Alexander (D-Ark.) spoke of "a disaster threatening to overtake the American farmer" while introducing a debt relief bill (3 February 1983, *Congressional Record*, 98th Congress, 295-301); Rep. Claude Pepper (D-Fla.) described "an economic crisis that threatens [farmers'] livelihoods and the system which provides . . . vital food and fiber" (10 Feb. 1983, *Congressional Record* 5841); and Rep. Byron L. Dorgan called for "action on the crisis in agriculture" (3 Feb. 1983, *Congressional Record* H420).

relevant articles from *Newsweek* and the *New York Times*. The *Times* said: "There is a real danger of a wave of farm bankruptcies, like those of the later 1920s, which could set off a similar ripple effect throughout the economy."[2] The article cited as evidence of distress the fact that Iowa land formerly selling for $3,000–$4,000 per acre "now goes for no more than $1,800." The other articles emphasized the threat of bankruptcy, with a *Times* leader on January 16, 1983, proclaiming "In farm belt, fear of foreclosure rises," and *Newsweek* citing a survey in which "fully 66 percent of those questioned feared losing their houses or farms within a year."[3]

There will always be a certain amount of gloom in politicians' and journalists' assessments of the farm economy, derived from farmers' own statements of their problems. However, the current economic status of U.S. farmers, although certainly worse than in the mid-1970s, is not one of crisis.

Consider farm income. Comparing total farm income today with that of the 1930s is misleading because there are many fewer farmers producing much more per farm; they receive lower prices, but they also incur lower real costs. In the past 50 years the number of U.S. farms has dropped from 6.5 million to just over 2 million, and total factor productivity (output per unit of real resources) has slightly more than doubled. Moreover, farmers today obtain more income from nonfarm sources than in the past and so are less dependent on commodity markets to determine their standard of living. The single best indicator of economic well-being is probably real income per farm family. In 1934, the first year in which the U.S. Department of Agriculture (USDA) kept farm income estimates comparable to current estimates, this figure was $3,200 (in 1972 dollars); in recent years it has been more than three times as high (table 1). Moreover, from 1940 to 1980 farmers have accumulated real net wealth at an even faster rate.

As of 1980, farms with less than $5,000 in annual sales accounted for 35 percent of the nation's 2.4 million farms—and $5,000 is the annual value of the output from two good cows or about fourteen acres of corn belt land. As commercial agricultural enterprises, these "farms" are trivial; in fact, the USDA estimates that in 1980 more than 95 percent of the income from such farms came from nonfarm sources. This nonfarm income amounted to $20,000 per farm; these small operations are in no sense poor, with an average net worth of $93,000.[4]

---

2. Seth S. King, "Farm Price Props Expected to Rise Above 1982 Record," *New York Times*, Jan. 27, 1983, p. 1.

3. 1 February 1983, *Congressional Record*, 98th Congress, 5841.

4. U.S. Department of Agriculture, Economic Research Service, *Economic Indicators of the Farm Sector*, Stat. Bul. No. 674 (Sept. 1981), p. 99.

TABLE 1

AVERAGE FINANCIAL STATUS OF U.S. FARMS

	Income, Assets, and Liabilities					
	Income (farm and nonfarm)	*Percentage from nonfarm sources*	*Assets[a]*	*Liabilities[a]*	*Net worth[a]*	*Liability to asset ratio*
1940	4.1	36.0	28.7	5.4	23.3	.189
1960	6.7	39.0	77.2	9.1	71.0	.118
1980	10.8	61.0	233.2	36.7	196.5	.157
1981	10.8	59.0	231.3	37.1	194.2	.160
1982	9.5[b]	62.0[b]	222.8	39.8	183.0	.179

SOURCES: *Economic Report of the President* (Washington, D.C.: Government Printing Office, 1983); U.S. Department of Agriculture, *Economic Indicators of the Farm Sector, 1981.*

NOTE: Figures given are in thousands of 1972 dollars; nominal values deflated by the GNP deflator.

a. As of January 1 of each year.
b. Author's estimate.

The farms that are significantly affected by commodity policy are those with $40,000 or more in sales. Some 27.5 percent of U.S. farms in 1980, these produced 88 percent of the value of products sold and showed an average net income of $34,700; 29 percent of that income came from nonfarm sources. Their mean assets were $714,000 which, with an average debt of $183,000, left their mean net worth at $531,000 in 1980. It is true that between 1980 and 1982, low farm prices eroded the net returns to and net worth of these farmers; but as a whole, U.S. commercial agriculture remains in excellent economic health.

These averages do obscure the very real financial difficulties faced by some large-scale farmers, whose farms may have been expanded recently through the purchase of high-priced land with relatively low down payments and big mortgages. Much of the concern about farmers pertains to this financially hard-pressed group. These farmers are in debt and they do face the threat of bankruptcy.

The data do not support any claim that foreclosures are rampant in farming. In 1982 the Farmers Home Administration (FmHA), lender to the shakiest farm enterprises, foreclosed on 844 loans, about 3.5 per 10,000 farm operators. When foreclosures by commercial lenders (which are also up sharply) are included, the rate of business failure in farming is below the rate for nonfarm businesses, which was about 6 per 1,000 in 1982.[5] On the whole, the 1980-82 recession was more serious for manufacturing than for farming.

More alarming is the fact that about 25 percent of FmHA loans are behind on their repayment schedules; however, this figure has hovered between 10 percent and 20 percent for the past several years.[6] The FmHA loan programs aid farmers who cannot obtain credit elsewhere, and collection policies are liberal. A major cause of FmHA repayment difficulties is the issuance of emergency FmHA credit in the late 1970s.[7] The Farm Credit Act of 1978 created a $6 billion loan program that enabled some economically fragile enterprises to remain in business for a few more years.

In 1980 and again in 1983, farmers in several important areas suffered severe losses from drought. Uninsured farmers who lost crops in several years faced a real threat of bankruptcy. Crop insurance is available to most farmers on liberal terms (including a 30 percent premium subsidy from the Federal Crop Insurance Corporation (FCIC) of the U.S. Department of Agriculture). Farmers in areas not covered by FCIC insurance were eligible for the Disaster Payment Program for major crops, which essentially provides free crop insurance in counties too risky even for the subsidized FCIC insurance. Thus, the farm sector is quite well protected from the financial consequences of crop failure.

Farmers were adversely affected by low crop prices and high interest rates in 1982 and by bad weather in 1983, but these phenomena did not constitute a general crisis. There was no need for special policy efforts to save or subsidize commercial agriculture. Discussion of agricultural policy should be based on its longer-term relationship to the economics of the U.S. farm sector.

Policy and Price Instability

Although it is questionable whether they have had any significant political influence, economists' theories about a possible "farm problem" should be mentioned here. The common elements of such theories involve the competitive nature of farm commodity markets, contrasted with imperfectly competitive middlemen, farm-supply industries, and nonagricultural product markets;

---

5. U.S. Council of Economic Advisers, *Economic Report of the President, 1982*, (Washington, D.C.: U.S. Government Printing Office), p. 268.

6. U.S. Department of Agriculture, "A Brief History of the Farmers Home Administration" (March 1982), p. 33.

7. The FmHA reports that staff years for loan processing and servicing declined from 2.3 per $1 million in 1962 to 0.19 per $1 million in 1981 (Ibid., p. 27), suggesting that less time has been spent on monitoring and collecting in recent years.

rapid technical progress in agriculture coupled with low income and price elasticity of demand for farm products; and immobile labor and fixed investment in agriculture. These conditions are said to generate a chronic disequilibrium characterized by an oversupply of farm products, weak prices, and low incomes.[8]

Although this model may have been useful from 1920 to 1970, it is quite doubtful that it is as helpful today. The general rate of return on labor and investment in agriculture is no longer out of line with comparable returns in the nonfarm sector.[9] More fundamentally, chronic overinvestment and excess labor in agriculture suggest not that price supports and related commodity market intervention are needed, but rather policies to promote labor mobility, improve rural schooling, and make market information and outlook services available.[10]

A need for stability is a more solid rationale for government intervention in the commodity markets. Since the 1970s there has been intensified study of considerations that favor intervention to stabilize grain markets, based on the domestic dynamics and unpredictabilities of supply, international trade and policy instabilities, and the macroeconomic consequences of agricultural price shocks.[11]

The policy actions most directly related to concerns about market price instability are trade liberalization and management of grain stocks. Although stabilization has been a stated objective of farm policy since Hoover's Federal Farm Board of 1929, the farm price and income support objective has dominated federal policy; consider the recurrent attempts to reduce federal stocks in a way that will not depress commodity prices, whereas in terms of stabilization a chief function of stocks is precisely to depress prices when they

---

8. See G.E. Brandow, "Policy for Commercial Agriculture," in Lee Martin, ed., *A Survey of Agricultural Economics Literature*, vol. 1 (Minneapolis: University of Minnesota Press, 1977).

9. See Luther Tweeten, "Farm Commodity Prices and Income," in B.L. Gardner and J.W. Richardson, eds., *Consensus and Conflict in U.S. Agriculture* (College Station, Texas: Texas A & M University Press, 1979); and B. Hottel and R. Reinsel, "Returns to Equity Capital by Economic Class of Farm," Agr. Econ. Report No. 347 (Washington, D.C.: U.S. Department of Agriculture Economic Research Service, 1976).

10. H. Houthakker, "Economic Policy for the Farm Sector" (Washington, D.C.: American Enterprise Institute, 1967); D.G. Johnson, *World Agriculture in Disarray* (London: Fontana/Collins, 1973); T.W. Schultz, *Economic Crises in World Agriculture* (Ann Arbor, Michigan: University of Michigan Press, 1965).

11. See, for example, T.E. Josling, "Interrelationships of Agricultural and General Economic Policies," in B. Dancy, T. Josling, and A. McFarquhar, eds., *Agriculture and the State* (London: Macmillan Press Ltd., 1976); K.L. Robinson, "Unstable Farm Prices," *American Journal of Agricultural Economics* (Dec. 1975); G.E. Schuh, "The New Macroeconomics of Agriculture," *American Journal of Agricultural Economics* (Dec. 1976); M.D. Bale and E. Lutz, "The Effects of Trade Intervention on International Price Instability," *American Journal of Agricultural Economics* (May 1979).

are abnormally high. Similarly, instead of using trade liberalization as a stabilizing force, agricultural exports have been promoted while imports have been discouraged to protect domestic producers. If the U.S. were to undertake pure stabilization policies, farmers might actually be made worse off.[12]

Restraints on exports of soybeans and grains were imposed on occasion between 1973 and 1975, but these actions had only a slight moderating effect on prices. The Carter administration's embargo of grain sales to the Soviets in 1980 was clearly a political effort to punish the Soviet Union for invading Afghanistan, as evidenced by simultaneous attempts to prevent U.S. farm prices from falling. These examples of actions that could lower farm prices were so strongly opposed by farm interests that it seems unlikely that similar efforts will be attempted frequently in the future.

Policy and Interest Groups

U.S. farm policies reflect deliberate congressional choices calibrated, like all such decisions, to political pressures. These policies have for fifty years consisted essentially of supply controls, production subsidies, and demand expansion.

Institutional mechanisms for controlling supplies, subsidizing production, and expanding markets (simultaneously in the case of grains and cotton) have varied widely in extent (see table 2). The real peak of federal intervention in agriculture occurred not in the New Deal but in the late 1950s and 1960s. A major shift occurred in the mid-1960s, when payments to farmers increased sharply but governmental stocks decreased (as, eventually, did acreage diversion). This period also saw a general trend toward lower real price support levels (fig. 1).

The general view among agricultural economists is that these support programs generated substantial income gains to farmers, but that the distribution of the gains among crop and livestock producers, large and small farms, landowners, tenants, and farm laborers has proved resistant to accurate estimation. There is general agreement, however, that the aggregate gains to producers of farm commodities are less than the costs to consumers and taxpayers. In a typical post-World War II year, a reasonable estimate is that agricultural support programs increased producers' net returns by $10 to $15 billion (1982 dollars) at a cost to consumers and taxpayers of $15 to $20 billion (including the costs of administering the programs through the Agricultural Stabilization and Conservation Service, but not the costs of farmers'

---

12. For detailed discussion, see R. Just, D. Hueth, and A. Schmitz, *Applied Welfare Economics* (Englewood Cliffs, N.J.: Prentice-Hall, 1982), ch. 11.

FIGURE 1

REAL SUPPORT PRICES AND MARKET PRICES: 11 CROP INDEX

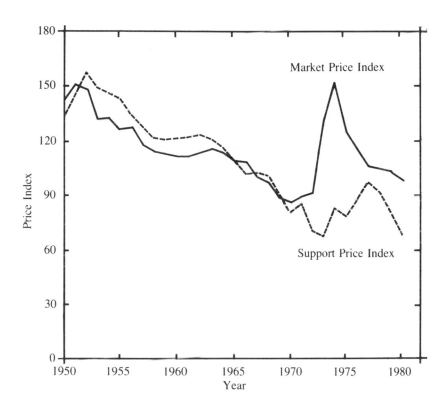

lobbying and counter-lobbying).[13] The difference comprises administrative costs, efficiency losses because of a product mix that does not allocate resources according to consumer demands, and the costs of idle land. The result is a deadweight loss of a few billion dollars per year, placing farm programs in the set of activities "silting up the stream," in Mancur Olson's phrase, of the American economy.[14]

---

13. The softness of these numbers should be emphasized. For further details, see Bruce Gardner, *The Governing of Agriculture* (Lawrence, Kansas: The Regents Press of Kansas, 1981).
14. Mancur Olson, *The Rise and Decline of Nations* (New Haven: Yale University Press, 1982).

TABLE 2

SOME AGGREGATE INDICATORS OF INTERVENTION IN AGRICULTURE

Year	Diverted Acres (Millions)	Government Year-End Stocks (Millions of 1967 Dollars)	Government Payments to Farmers (Millions of 1967 Dollars)
1933	0	0	337
1934	35	0	1,112
1935	30	0	1,394
1936	31	0	669
1937	26	0	781
1938	0	21	1,056
1939	0	26	1,834
1940	0	1,126	1,721
1941	0	1,646	1,233
1942	0	1,389	1,331
1943	0	1,729	1,245
1944	0	1,633	1,472
1945	0	1,710	1,376
1946	0	837	1,319
1947	0	439	469
1948	0	208	356
1949	0	1,515	259
1950	0	3,639	392
1951	0	1,841	367
1952	0	1,349	345
1953	0	2,694	265
1954	0	4,260	319
1955	0	5,700	285
1956	14	6,614	680
1957	28	5,620	1,205
1958	27	5,430	1,257
1959	22	6,024	781
1960	28	6,788	791
1961	53	6,208	1,666
1962	64	4,938	1,928
1963	56	5,153	1,849
1964	55	4,963	2,347
1965	57	4,349	2,606
1966	63	2,407	3,371
1967	40	1,005	3,079
1968	49	1,021	3,322
1969	58	1,624	3,455
1970	57	1,370	3,196
1971	37	921	2,592
1972	62	662	3,161

TABLE 2 *(continued)*

Year	Diverted Acres (Millions)	Government Year-End Stocks (Millions of 1967 Dollars)	Government Payments to Farmers (Millions of 1967 Dollars)
1973	19	296	1,958
1974	3	127	359
1975	2	249	500
1976	2	371	430
1977	0	608	1,002
1978	16	606	1,550
1979	11	570	647
1980	0	1,134	515

SOURCES: U.S. Department of Agriculture; U.S. Council of Economic Advisers.

Part of the reason for the trend toward lower support prices and less intervention in the 1960s and 1970s was a growing perception that farmers were not receiving nearly as much from farm programs as consumers and taxpayers were paying. Evidence for this is most abundant in the analyses and budget proposals emanating from the executive branch; presidents from Eisenhower through Carter sought ways to reduce the scope of farm programs.[15] Congress, on the other hand, has been more resistant to reform of agricultural policy under both Democratic and Republican control.

The Reagan Administration's Agricultural Policies

Ronald Reagan evinced little interest in agricultural policy during the presidential campaign of 1980. In this he followed the tradition of every twentieth-century president (with the possible exception of Jimmy Carter). With no particular vision of what agricultural policy ought to be, the Reagan administration apparently let its laissez-faire beliefs govern its agricultural policy positions in early decision making. This was exemplified by statements of Secretary of Agriculture John Block in early 1981 to the effect that farming ought to be as free of government intervention as possible.

The administration's general view that the federal government should do less in agriculture, in the absence of a particular theory of why it should do less,

---

15. See the sections on agriculture in past annual issues of the *Economic Report of the President*, for example, 1962, 1965, 1974, 1975, 1977, 1981.

has caused problems in policy making. The administration's first agricultural policy pronouncements involved calls for restraint on dairy support prices, phase-outs of the target prices and deficiency payments for grain and cotton, and changes in the acreage-control programs for peanuts and tobacco. These positions were not notably different from those of the Nixon, Ford, or Carter administrations. The main changes in agricultural policy early in the Reagan administration were the freeze on the milk support price in April 1981 and the end of the embargo on shipments of U.S. grain to the Soviet Union.

The Reagan administration's first important opportunity to influence the laws governing U.S. agriculture policy came up during debate on the Agriculture and Food Act of 1981. The administration did not press for the changes in peanut and sugar legislation it favored, probably as part of its bargaining efforts for tax and spending policies; nonetheless, the 1981 act was perceived as austere, reflecting administration pressures to keep budgetary costs down.[16]

Such costs, however, only partly indicate the extent of governmental involvement in agriculture. The tobacco program operates at almost zero budgetary cost, indeed is required to do so by the Agriculture and Food Act of 1981, yet tobacco growers are heavily protected—output quotas make the industry an effective cartel. Acreage reduction programs can reduce government price support and deficiency payment for grain, but only by increasing the prices paid by grain users. And there is an inevitable resource cost in the idling of productive cropland.

The best single indicator of changes in the level of protection of commodity markets is the price level established for farmers, whether guaranteed by deficiency payments, Commodity Credit Corporation (CCC) purchases, or acreage cutbacks. Support prices for corn, wheat, milk, and cotton (see table 3) do not suggest the austere farm policy that the 1981 act was supposed to have represented. The incentive prices for farmers, best measured by the target prices for grains, rice, and cotton, were all increased in real terms by the 1981 act (compare the 1983 figures with those of 1980).

Real support prices for these commodities followed a general downward trend from the mid-1950s to the mid-1970s. Toward the end of the period, cash payments to producers tended to replace government purchases. The cash payments, however, were made on only a fraction of historical production, such as the domestic allotment for wheat. This buffered, although it

---

16. See C.L. Infanger, W.C. Bailey, and D.R. Dyer, "Agricultural Policy in Austerity: The Making of the 1981 Farm Bill," *American Journal of Agricultural Economics* (February 1983), pp. 1–9; F.H. Sanderson, "U.S. Farm Policy in Perspective," *Food Policy* (February 1983), pp. 3–12; S.H. Hargrove, "The Agriculture and Food Act of 1981," (New York: Peat, Marwick, Mitchell & Company, 1982).

TABLE 3

REAL SUPPORT PRICES
(1972 Dollars)

Crop Year	Corn ($ per bu.)	Wheat ($ per bu.)	Cotton (¢ per lb.)	Milk (¢ per lb.)
1970[a]	1.09	1.31	21.1	5.12
1971[a]	1.05	1.25	19.5	5.13
1972[a]	.99	1.18	18.4	5.00
Mean:	1.04	1.25	19.7	5.08
1977	1.33	1.93	31.9	6.57
1978	1.29	2.09	31.9	6.89
1979	1.24	1.92	32.6	7.31
1980	1.21	1.87	30.1	6.98
Mean:	1.27	1.95	31.6	6.94
1981	1.18	1.85	34.7	6.75
1982	1.27	1.90	33.3	6.42
1983	1.30	1.95	34.5	6.15
Mean:	1.25	1.90	34.2	6.44
Percentage Changes				
1970–72 to 1977–80	22	56	60	37
1977–80 to 1981–83	−2	−3	8	−7

SOURCE: U.S. Department of Agriculture, *Agricultural Statistics* (Washington, D.C.: U.S. Government Printing Office), various issues.

a. These prices are market support prices (loan rates) and exclude payments made on intramarginal acreage for grains and cotton.

probably did not eliminate, the incentive for producers to respond to payments by increasing output.

A significant change occurred with the Food and Agriculture Act of 1977, which governed policy during the Carter administration. The 1977 act based payments on each farmer's current production level. The payment was determined by the difference between a legislated "target" price and the actual U.S. average market price. This essentially guaranteed the average farmer the target price.

The producer prices established for crops harvested in 1977 and thereafter were substantially above previous support prices. This was not considered likely to create an incentive to production while the 1977 act was being developed, because real market prices had been well above the new target prices throughout the mid-1970s. This led policy makers to assume that market prices would remain above the support prices. However, prices declined in 1977, and in 1978 and 1979 the Carter administration found it necessary to reintroduce set-asides (requirements that farmers not plant 10 percent to 20 percent of normal crop acreage in order to qualify for deficiency payments). The larger surpluses of 1981 and 1982 have been attributed to favorable weather, and the policy problems of the early 1980s might be seen as an unfortunate but unforeseeable accident; but it was inevitable that favorable weather should occur sometime. Actually, grain yields have not been far out of line with long-term trends (fig. 2).

The demand for U.S. grain has been weakened by expanded production abroad, by the appreciation of the dollar, and by the worldwide recession. Nonetheless, the fundamental reason for current policy problems is that the incentive prices in the grain programs are too high, causing a tendency to

FIGURE 2

U.S. FEED GRAIN YIELD PER HARVESTED ACRE

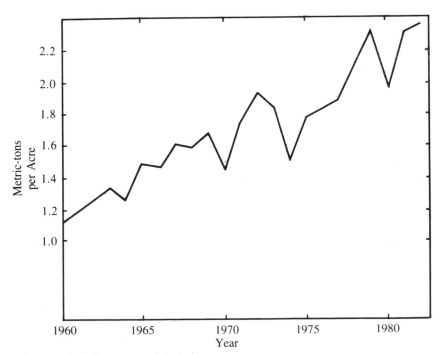

SOURCE: U.S. Department of Agriculture.

overproduce that no prospective weakening of the dollar or worldwide recovery is likely to offset for long.

Large budgetary outlays and stocks of grain led to the Reagan administration's main policy thrust in late 1982 and 1983. In its first budget projections for fiscal year 1983, the administration projected outlays for commodity programs (primarily payments to farmers, costs of stored commodities, and costs of subsidized sales of surplus products at home and abroad) of less than $2 billion. By early 1982, that figure had been revised to $5 billion to $6 billion, and in mid-1983 it became apparent that actual outlays would be in the neighborhood of $21 billion. Although this last figure is not much higher than the outlays of the 1960s in real dollar terms, the size of these costs has been and continues to be a cause of consternation to the administration. If these outlays were thought to be only transitory, perhaps to decline in 1984, they would probably not have led to significant policy changes. The accumulation of stocks was more important.

Production and domestic use of corn increased steadily from 1964 to 1983, and exports grew rapidly (table 4). Stocks accumulated periodically, but were not an unusually high percentage of trend production until 1981–1982, when ending stocks of 2.3 billion bushels were 28 percent of 1981 production; consequently, the administration established a modest acreage restraint program for the 1982 crops.

In August and September 1982 the Reagan administration announced several main features of its 1983 program. Details of the programs for wheat, corn, barley, sorghum, oats, rice, and cotton varied, but the essential features of the program were the same for all.

The 1983 grain and cotton programs gave renewed emphasis to production controls. Production controls were attractive because, given the projection that the market price for 1983 corn would be at the CCC support price and that considerable stocks would be accumulated, the government would save twenty-one cents per bushel in deficiency payments and the costs of acquiring CCC grain if production could be reduced sufficiently to increase the market price above the target price level. These costs could easily amount to $3 billion for corn.

The corn production control measures, announced in September 1982, included a 10 percent acreage reduction requirement for deficiency payments or CCC loans. Acreage reduction is costly to the farmer because the acreage produces nothing and there may also be added costs of planting a cover crop. The basic opportunity cost to the farmer is the return that could have been earned if the land had been in production.

The economics of the farmer's decision to participate is best shown by an example. Consider a farmer with ten acres, yielding 100 bushels of corn

TABLE 4

U.S. CORN SUPPLY AND UTILIZATION
(Millions of Bushels)

| Crop Year (Beginning October) | Supply | | Demand | | |
	Beginning Stocks	Production	Domestic Use	Exports	Ending Stocks
1964–65	1,537	3,484	3,305	570	1,147
1965–66	1,147	4,103	3,722	687	842
1966–67	842	4,168	3,698	487	826
1967–68	826	4,860	3,885	633	1,169
1968–69	1,169	4,450	3,966	536	1,118
1969–70	1,118	4,687	4,189	612	1,005
1970–71	1,005	4,152	3,877	517	667
1971–72	667	5,646	4,391	796	1,127
1972–73	1,127	5,580	4,742	1,258	708
1973–74	708	5,671	4,653	1,243	484
1974–75	484	4,701	3,677	1,149	361
1975–76	361	5,829	4,082	1,711	399
1976–77	399	6,266	4,100	1,684	884
1977–78	884	6,505	4,334	1,948	1,111
1978–79	1,111	7,268	4,944	2,133	1,304
1979–80	1,304	7,938	5,193	2,433	1,618
1980–81	1,618	6,645	4,874	2,355	1,034
1981–82	1,034	8,201	5,085	2,075	2,289
1982–83[a]	2,076	8,315	5,251	2,350	2,791
1982–83[b]	2,289	8,397	5,200	2,100	3,384

SOURCE: U.S. Department of Agriculture, *Agricultural Statistics* (Washington, D.C.: U.S. Government Printing Office), various issues.
  a.   USDA projection, August 1982.
  b.   USDA estimate, March 1983.

per acre. If the farmer does not participate in the program, the revenue earned is determined by the market price. It would be reasonable to expect this price to be at or near the market support price, determined by the loan rate of $2.65 per bushel. Therefore expected revenue on ten acres for the non-participant would be $2.65 × 1000 bu. = $2,650. A participant earns no revenue on one set-aside acre but is guaranteed the target price of $2.86 per bushel on the nine remaining acres. Thus, expected revenue is $2.86 × 900 bu. = $2,574. Expected revenue is less by $76, but costs are also reduced for the participant by the variable costs of growing one acre of corn, which is likely to be fairly close to $76 per acre. Because the incentive for participation is not great, participation in such acreage reduction or set-aside programs has usually not been high. The usual participants are farmers who have land that they do not wish to farm in any case, or poor land that has had a program yield far above its actual expected yield.

To encourage participation, a 10 percent voluntary paid diversion feature was added to the 1983 program. This additional 10 percent idling of land is encouraged by a payment of $1.50 per bushel that could have been grown on the land had it been used in production and generated the program yield. If program yield were 100 bushels per acre, as in the example, the producer would receive $150 per acre placed in this program; and, under the assumption that the opportunity cost of the idle land and associated fixed factors is less than $150 per acre, this paid diversion feature is profitable and participation is more likely. However, a farmer cannot be in the paid diversion program without also being in the acreage reduction program, and this dilutes the incentive to participate.

The Birth of PIK

After the September 1982 announcement of 1983 programs, evidence accumulated that ending stocks in fall 1983 would be even larger than had been anticipated. Compare the USDA projections of August 1982 with those of March 1983 (table 4). Production had been revised upward slightly, the carry-over from the preceding crop year had also been revised upward, domestic use had been revised slightly downward and exports substantially downward, adding up to a projection for ending stocks for 1982 that was about 600 million bushels higher than was thought in August 1982. This revision suggested that more drastic production control measures should be tried.

These measures took the form of the administration's Payment in Kind (PIK) program. Under this program, a producer who had agreed to place 20 percent of his other 1982 corn base acreage in the acreage reduction and diversion programs became eligible to idle another 10 percent to 30 percent of acreage. The payment for idling this land was to be made not in dollars but in kind (i.e., corn) and was to consist of 80 percent of the corn that could have been produced on the idle land. In the example, the producer would receive eighty bushels for every acre idled; at the loan rate of $2.65 per bushel, this payment would be $212 per acre. Because the cost of idling the land is $80 per acre, PIK offers a very substantial net gain to the farmer. A producer could also submit a sealed bid offering to divert all of his or her land if paid a percentage of normal yield (up to 80 percent) chosen by the producer.

The USDA's estimate is that 82 million acres were idled under 1983 programs for all crops. This makes the Reagan administration custodian of the largest acreage diversion program ever—by nearly 30 percent (see table 2 for data on earlier diversion programs). The estimate is that 52 million acres of corn were harvested, which is a 29 percent reduction from 1982 corn acreage. The PIK program, more than the drought of July and August 1983, is responsible for the 48 percent reduction in the 1983 corn crop (compared with the 1982 crop).

Evaluating PIK and Other Programs

While explaining to Congress the rationale for the PIK program, Secretary of Agriculture Block cited the following causes of the weak markets of 1982: record production of major crops in 1981–1982 and 1982–1983; the embargo on exports of U.S. grain to the Soviet Union; global recession; the strong dollar; barriers to the importation of U.S. agricultural products and subsidized exports by the European Economic Community and Japan, and the financial problems of major importers of U.S. farm products. All these factors dramatically reduced the prices received by farmers. Block stated that "the key to improved price and farm income prospects is to take the necessary steps to get supplies more nearly into balance with demand."[17] The PIK program, it was said, would reduce production and accumulated stocks while keeping grain available for export; it would also reduce governmental outlays, be self-terminating "when excessive stocks have been worked off," and maintain farmers' returns.[18] As complementary policy steps, Block mentioned the distribution of surplus grain abroad and a freeze on target prices for future years.

The issues to be considered here are how well PIK could be expected to deal with the underlying causes of the farm problem, and whether the improvement of farm price and income prospects through PIK is a wise policy. Consider what effects PIK and related programs can be expected to have (neglecting the underlying causes of recent commodity price weaknesses, and taking existing supply and demand conditions as constraints within which 1983 commodity policy must be conducted).

Data for the past decade's corn prices and quantities—corn being the key commodity under current policy—are shown in figure 3. Quantity figures come from USDA supply data (table 4) and include production plus beginning stocks. So measured, supply equals total demand—the sum of domestic use, exports, and ending stocks. Thus, the point labeled "82" shows the large supply available for 1982–83, priced at the CCC support level.

17. Statement of Secretary of Agriculture John R. Block before a subcommittee of the Senate Agriculture Committee, U.S. Senate, 97th Congress, 2d sess., Dec. 9, 1982.

18. Ibid., p. 4.

FIGURE 3

CORN PRICE AND SUPPLY, 1973–82

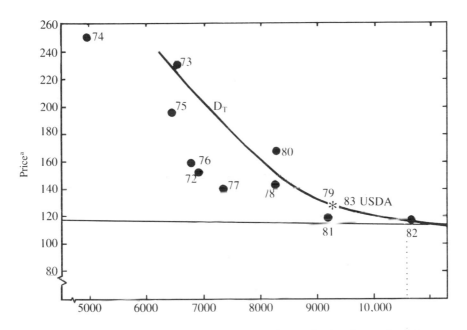

a. In 1972 dollars per bushel. Prices are average prices received by farmers for each crop year, deflated by the GNP deflator (1972 = 100). The crop year starts October 1 of the date plotted. Thus, the point labelled "80" is the average farm price for the period October 1, 1980 to September 30, 1981.

It would be unfair to base an evaluation of PIK on hindsight, and this assessment is based on information available early in 1983. Generally, PIK and related programs were expected to have two direct effects: first, to reduce the 1983 supply as compared with that of 1982; second, to shift the ownership of stocks from the CCC to farmers. The USDA's forecast of the size of the supply reduction was from 10.7 billion bushels to 9.1 billion bushels, or about 15 percent, with a corresponding real price increase of about 10 percent.[19] The projected equilibrium point ("83 USDA" in figure 3) shows much less

19. U.S. Department of Agriculture, "World Agricultural Supply and Demand Estimates," 147-7 (March 1983). The nominal projected price increase is from $2.55 per bushel in 1982/83 to a midpoint in estimated range of $2.90 per bushel in 1983/84, or a 14 percent increase. Subtracting an inflation rate of 4 percent yields a 10 percent real price rise.

price response to reduced supply than is thought usual for grains. If the 1982–83 and 1983–84 points were to lie on the same total demand curve, labeled D_T, it would have an elasticity of -1.5, while econometric studies of the corn market more typically find an elasticity in the neighborhood of -0.5. The -0.5 would imply a real price increase of 30 percent instead of 10 percent because of PIK.

The main reason to doubt forecasts based only on demand elasticity is that it is unlikely the 1983–84 demand for U.S. corn would be the same as it was in 1982–83. Export demand is quite unpredictable, but there seemed no reason to predict that it would be weaker in 1983-84 than it was in 1982–83. The USDA's early 1983 forecast was for slightly greater exports in 1983–84, for corn and for all grains, even at higher (U.S.) prices, and for slightly lower feed and other domestic use of corn than in 1982–83, but not enough to constitute any significant shift in demand. What about the demand for ending stocks out of 1983 supplies? This component of demand is most difficult of all to predict, depending as it does on current prices but also on expectations of future price gains, which are the returns for holding stocks.

In this respect the second feature of PIK, the transfer of stocks to farmers, becomes crucial. If their demand for stocks is much lower than the amount that the CCC's storage policies generate, the total demand for 1983–84 corn (and other grains) could well be reduced enough to make the demand curve D_T appropriate; in which case the ''83 USDA'' projection would be a reasonable forecast.[20]

Econometric models of agricultural commodity markets developed in the past ten years could also have been used to make forecasts; however, these models, while containing a wealth of detail about farmers' supply responses and livestock-feed technical relationships, are weak in specifying, much less forecasting, export demand and demand for stocks by farmers. They consequently have little to contribute to a forecast of PIK effects on prices.

The main uncertainty is the level of supply and foreign demand, which cannot be reliably forecast without information on weather in the United States and abroad. U.S. production is also uncertain because the effects of PIK on yield per acre are not surely known. The USDA's projection prior to knowledge of 1983 growing-season weather was that feed grain yield would be

---

20. Some have suggested that the increase in stocks that are in farmers' hands and not part of any storage program could reduce cash prices, although it would increase expected future prices. (See T. Oppenheimer, ''Reagan's Surplus Crop Scheme Could Founder if Farmers Rush to Market,'' *National Journal* (March 5, 1983), pp. 507–510; L. Tweeten, ''Policy Alternatives for Wheat,'' presented at Farmers Agricultural Policy Conference, Stillwater, Okla., Nov. 12, 1982.) However, the announcement of PIK in late 1982 and its successful sign-up period in 1983 seemed to have strengthened both near and distant futures prices about equally.

about 2.38 metric tons per harvest acre, or about 3.50 percent above trend yield for 1983.[21] The yield was actually 2.05 metric tons per harvested acre, about 14 percent less than had been expected.

Social and Other Costs

When PIK decisions were made, the uncertainties were such that the price of corn could have been anywhere from zero to 40 percent higher in 1983-84 under the Reagan administration's farm programs, than if there were neither production controls nor PIK (but assuming the legislated target price, loan rate, and grain storage programs). The best estimate of the price effect was in the middle of this range. For other feed grains, the magnitude of the price change would be about the same; for wheat a smaller price impact could be expected, and for rice and cotton, a larger one.

Who pays these higher prices, and what consequences do they have? Consider the two extremes of a zero and a 40 percent increase in the price of corn. If there were no price increases, stocks would be reduced but there would be no induced adjustment in consumption or exports; thus, the policy-induced reduction in stocks in 1984 would equal the policy-induced production cutback. The USDA projected this to be about 2.7 billion bushels, or one-third of 1982 corn production—93 million metric tons (mmt) or 27 percent of 1982 production, for all grains and rice.[22]

The budgetary cost of achieving this reduction in government-held stocks is several billion dollars in cash acreage diversion and PIK payments, less several billion dollars that the CCC would otherwise have spent on loans and purchases of commodities and deficiency payments. There is a net saving to the U.S. Treasury if the grain that could have been produced and stored in 1983 were regarded as valueless, and this seems to be USDA's view.[23] However, the expected real gain to farmers from PIK is predicated on the fact that the grain they are given is valuable. In these calculations the price of grain is assumed not to rise because of PIK; shouldn't the market price be used to value CCC-owned grain? The answer is no, because the market price would be at an artificially high supported level, especially at 1983 production

---

21. Based on a 1983 trend yield of 2.3 metric tons per acre, from figure 2 and from analysis of Luther Tweeten, "Excess Farm Supply: Permanent or Transitory?" paper presented at the National Agricultural Policy Symposium, Kansas City (March 1983).

22. U.S. Department of Agriculture, *World Agricultural Supply and Demand Estimates* (March 1983), WASDE-155.

23. Oppenheimer ("Reagan's Surplus Crop Scheme") quotes a USDA official as saying that PIK grain is "really an asset with no value." This view seems also to lie behind the discussion in U.S. Department of Agriculture, Economic Research Service, "An Initial Assessment of the Payment-in-Kind Program" (April 1983) p. 20.

levels in the absence of PIK. The economic value of stockpiled grain would be lower.

How much lower? Suppose that the expected supply, without PIK, of all grains in 1983–84 would have been 485 mmt (1983 carry-out stocks plus 1984 production at almost 1983 levels). This would be a 10 percent increase over a level that was itself about 10 percent higher than the level at which the unregulated market price would be at the loan rate. With an elasticity of demand for total grains of -0.5, the "real" value of grains would be roughly 40 percent less than the loan rates. On this basis it can be estimated that the expected real social value of the 93 mmt of grains not produced in 1983 was about $80 per metric ton, or about $7.5 billion. There are some savings of resources that would have been used to produce this grain, such as fuel, fertilizer, and other variable costs; but the services of idled land and associated fixed factors—some equipment, machinery, and infrastructure services, and operator labor and management—would be irretrievably lost. If these amount to $65 per acre,[24] the idling of 80 million acres in 1983 will have a net resource cost of about $5 billion.

Stored grain is a risky asset, and this $7.5 billion estimate is really an expected value. There might be a 30 percent chance that four years or more would pass before real prices rose sufficiently to sell the grain at 10 percent above the loan rate. Considering storage costs during that period, the present discounted value of the stored grain would be close to zero. On the other hand, there is perhaps a 20 percent chance during the 1980s of a substantial shortfall in agricultural production, with real prices doubling or tripling in a short period, and in this case, the present value of stored grain could be very high. For example, in 1970 a billion bushels of CCC corn was also implicitly treated as valueless by the government; but in retrospect, the present value of grain stored in 1970 for sale in 1974, say, was on the order of twice the 1970 loan rate. It is by no means implausible to value grain that could be produced in 1983 for CCC storage at 60 percent or so of the loan rate instead of zero. The U.S. corn yield decline from 114 bushels per acre in 1982, a decline of 25 percent, is evidence that the picture can indeed change rapidly.

The preceding analysis has assumed that the administration's PIK plan would not raise grain prices. Suppose the price of corn, and of all grains taken together, rose by 40 percent (an outcome more nearly correct than USDA's early 1983 projection). This is much more favorable to farmers—

---

24. This assumes that the 80 million acres enrolled for grains and rice has a rental value of $50 per acre (this is lower than the corresponding value for U.S. cropland, which is closer to $70, because less productive land will be diverted) and that associated idled inputs have a value of $15 per acre.

they receive the same acreage diversion payments as before, and both their home-grown and government-given grain would be 40 percent more valuable. Even a net price increase of 20 percent would mean about a $10 billion gain, with another $5 billion or so as the value of PIK grain and payments less the costs of idled land. Thus, this scenario generates a $15 billion net income gain for farmers, or about $7,000 per farm.

What is the probability of a shortage severe enough to raise grain prices by 40 percent? The world supply-demand balance (see table 5) is of primary importance here. Although stocks are high, two successive years of world grain production one standard deviation below trend would probably make those stocks valuable, and the probability of this event occurring in the next five years could well be 20 percent.

In terms of the federal budget, it would be better if prices rose because about $4 billion in deficiency payments would be avoided; little grain would be placed under CCC loan and not redeemed by farmers. Higher grain prices also remove some of the incentives for dairy production and reduce the budgetary cost of the dairy price support program. However, these items involve no real net gain to society. They simply replace transfer payments from taxpayers to grain producers by a larger transfer from grain consumers to grain producers. The net resource cost of PIK is actually higher if prices rise because the social value of the grain not produced in 1983 is higher.

TABLE 5

WORLD GRAIN SUPPLY-DEMAND BALANCE

		Wheat and Feed Grains (Millions of Metric Tons)				
	Beginning Stocks	*Production*	*Supply*	*Consumption*	*Ending Stocks*	*Stock/Utili-zation Ratio*
1978–79	170	1,200	1,370	1,178	192	0.16
1979–80	192	1,164	1,356	1,184	172	0.15
1980–81	172	1,169	1,341	1,186	156	0.13
1981–82	156	1,226	1,382	1,190	195	0.16
1982–83[a]	192	1,229	1,421	1,206	215	0.15
1982–83[b]	192	1,260	1,452	1,207	249	0.21
1982–83[c]	200	1,259	1,459	1,215	244	0.20
1983–84[c]	244	1,164	1,408	1,232	177	0.13

SOURCE: U.S. Department of Agriculture, *Foreign Agriculture Circular: Grains* (Washington, D.C.: USDA), various issues.
  a.   August 1982 projection.
  b.   March 1983 estimate.
  c.   September 1983 estimate.

Thus, both a zero and a 40 percent rise in the price of corn (and pre-sumably all figures between these) suggest that PIK carries substantial social resource costs. The smallest net cost is on the order of $4 billion, and occurs only if PIK does not raise grain prices. If PIK does raise prices, the social costs are somewhat higher.

It might be argued that although $4 billion is a large social cost, it is nonetheless smaller than the cost of maintaining the price support levels in the Agriculture and Food Act of 1981 without production controls. The Reagan administration appears to have taken this view. Nonetheless, when considered as of early 1983, the probable value of the stocks that would have been forthcoming in the absence of PIK exceeded the value of the unused (seed, etc.) resources. This would have been the case even if 1983 were a normal production year. With the low actual yields of 1983, the case for growing crops instead of idling land is even stronger.

Without the PIK program, and under expectations as of early 1983, the legislated target price for corn of $2.86 per bushel meant that the nation would have used $2.86 in resources to produce corn with a marginal social value of about $1.70. The resulting estimate of deadweight loss is about $2 billion. The production cutback under PIK would have been a good social investment if all the resources used to produce the marginal 2.3 billion bushels of corn had been shifted to other uses; but the acreage reduction programs do not do this.

The calculation of the savings that are associated with lower production is especially difficult because of the magnitude of PIK. For example, hybrid seed is a variable cost in the usual accounting, but in 1983 so much less seed was used that its value has fallen substantially, and the value of the seed "saved" by PIK is less than its value in USDA's cost-of-production estimates. Meanwhile, the cost of seed for clover and other cover crops has in some cases tripled because of increased demand, and the net costs of the cover crops must be subtracted from the resource savings on PIK land. Fertilizers and pesticides are subject to similar, although not so severe, pressures. Ser-vices of machinery—particularly the capital tied up in them—will also be idled; and the only real machinery cost savings are fuel and maintenance. Consequently, the real resource savings from PIK are only about $0.70 per bushel, instead of the roughly $1.00 that USDA's cost-of-production figures typically suggest.

This means that PIK is saving about $1.6 billion in resources, while the value of unproduced corn (with an average social value of about $1.95 per bushel) is roughly $4.5 billion. The PIK program thus involves about $3 billion in deadweight loss in corn. (This figure would be roughly doubled for all grains, rice, and cotton as an aggregate.) This is about $1 billion more than the $2 billion deadweight loss that would have resulted if there had been no acreage controls in 1983.

The PIK program was a mistake, not only because it was likely to increase expected deadweight losses by perhaps a billion dollars, but also because of its effect on the farm-supply industries and the signals it sent to commodity producers and to grain-producing countries abroad. The program tells U.S. farmers that the federal government will take the necessary steps to maintain prices near target-price levels. Therefore, on acres that are not in the PIK program, farmers will continue to apply fertilizer, pesticides, water, and so forth as if the value of the output were at or above the target price. Over the longer term, the signals do nothing to discourage marginal producers from continuing to invest in their land by, for example, building irrigation or drainage systems.

The fundamental problem with the corn program is the pegging of the target price at $2.86, which leads (under normal weather and demand conditions) to the production of almost a half billion bushels above the quantity demanded at that price. As a policy response there is no good substitute for moving the target price down toward the long-term market-clearing level, which is probably about $2.60. The administration has indeed requested authority from Congress to hold the target price constant, which amounts to a real cut of about 4 percent per year at current inflation rates; but in the meantime, PIK signifies that every attempt will be made to defend the current farm support levels.

Production controls send an especially counterproductive signal to foreign grain producers. The United States' willingness to restrict production to maintain a world price at this level means that foreign producers can expand production with less fear of competition from U.S. supplies. (This threat is more serious for wheat and cotton than for corn, however.) The risk to the United States is one of either bigger surpluses or more PIK-like programs—in the extreme case, until the export market disappears.

In the longer term, the grain industries resemble the dairy industry in that the market-clearing price is below the support level. The U.S. dairy industry has already been isolated from world markets by import quotas on dairy products. A production control approach seems better suited to the milk market, because the long-run demand for milk is probably less elastic than demand for grain and because the economic value of the milk the government now holds is probably lower relative to future price prospects than the value of grains. Yet the Reagan administration has resisted pressures to reduce milk production; instead it has placed emphasis on reducing the support price level. The administration obtained legislation for an effective 4 percent reduction of about the same size in December 1982, with further reduction of about the same size implemented in the summer of 1983. This approach should have been used for grains and cotton.

In considering long-term policy, it is important to have the best possible information about the trend of market-clearing prices. For the dairy industry, the trend appears to be down; the likelihood of stronger demand is not as apparent as the likelihood of productivity gains that will increase supply. For grains, there are supportable arguments for both rising or falling prices in the longer term. Since the mid-1970s, expert opinion has swung toward thinking increasing prices more likely, but current surpluses suggest that the long-term trend toward lower real grain prices (a fall of about 1 percent per year in this century) was not reversed in the 1970s after all. A recent assessment indicates no predictable trend, up or down, for the remainder of this century, but substantial year-to-year fluctuation.[25] This reinforces the recommendation that current policy should emphasize obtaining the 15 percent or so reduction in target prices that the economic realities call for, without abandoning stock-holding as a policy tool.

Beyond PIK

With the exception of worldwide record yields, the administration's PIK program does not address the factors that Secretary of Agriculture Block cited as causing depressed prices in 1982–1983. The global recession, the strong dollar, and the financial difficulties of importing countries cannot be manipulated through U.S. agricultural policy. Grain export embargoes by the United States and agricultural protection by foreign governments do call for a policy response, and it is not clear how they can be dealt with by a laissez faire policy in agriculture.

The Reagan administration lifted President Carter's embargo of January 1980 on the Soviet Union's purchase of U.S. grain and has declared firmly its intent not to take such actions (although surely there are circumstances under which embargoes would occur again). It is doubtful that President Carter's embargo was a significant cause of the grain industries' problems today. In the short term, other suppliers appear to have filled the gaps created by the embargo in 1980. If the Soviets found and imported approximately as much wheat as they desired, the world supply/demand balance and so world prices should have been unchanged except for some forcing of inefficient shipping patterns.

The long-term effect of the embargo, which is said to have influenced 1982–83 prices, was to encourage the Soviets and others to regard the United

---

25. Tweeten, "Excess Farm Supply."

States as an unreliable supplier and to prefer purchasing from other countries, and certainly the Soviets, among others, would be prudent in diversifying their sources of supply. But how much of a premium would they pay to buy grain from a source other than the United States? Paying a significant premium seems unreasonable; and if the transfer of Soviet business to, for example, Argentina, did make U.S. grain cheaper, it would then be a better bargain for non-Soviet importers. Thus, data on the share of Soviet imports supplied by the United States are irrelevant. The real question is whether the price of grain from other countries rose relative to U.S. grain prices following the embargo. The data suggest that Argentinian corn and perhaps Canadian wheat did earn a premium in 1980, but that this did not persist (see table 6). These few calculations are by no means conclusive, but they do suggest that the Secretary of Agriculture might wish to adduce some evidence that the Carter embargo is a cause of current U.S. grain price weakness.[26]

On economic grounds, there is no case for subsidizing U.S. agricultural exports while not subsidizing domestic consumption, which the administration has chosen to do on several occasions. It can be argued that the 1982 cheese distribution program, for example, was a cost-effective way of eliminating inventories, expanding demand by offering lower prices. It might even be appropriate to offer more general consumer subsidies of surplus products, converting the dairy program to a de facto target price and deficiency payment basis with consumers receiving the payments in kind rather than producers in cash. This is preferable to selling products abroad at lower prices than at home because the well-being of U.S. consumers can be increased, at no net resource cost, by transferring goods from the foreign to the domestic market. The Department of Agriculture and the Office of Management and Budget prefer to subsidize foreign consumption because the budgetary cost per unit of additional demand is probably lower for foreign shipments, especially in the form of food aid.

A better defense of export subsidies is that they are necessary to make the threat of future subsidies convincing—this threat being a tool with which to persuade other countries to loosen their restrictive practices. Note that PIK is the opposite of a threat of export subsidy—it creates room for other countries' export expansion. Therefore a strategic argument for export subsidies is a strategic argument against PIK. On the other hand, a policy involving

---

26. See also, a recent report by the Joint Committee of Congress, which cites only data on the U.S. share of Soviet grain imports to support a claim that "international politics add to U.S. agriculture's predicament." ("The Changing Economics of Agriculture: Challenge and Preparation for the 1980s," A Staff Study for the JEC [Washington, D.C.: U.S. Government Printing Office], Dec. 28, 1982), pp. 14–15).

TABLE 6

INTERNATIONAL GRAIN PRICE RATIOS

	Wheat[a] (Canada/United States)	Corn[b] (Argentina/United States)
1975	1.21	1.03
1976	1.11	0.99
1977	1.10	0.95
1978	1.02	0.97
1979	1.06	0.99
1980	1.09	1.23
1981	1.11	1.03
1982	1.02	0.99

SOURCE: U.S. Department of Agriculture, *World Agriculture Outlook and Situation*, WAS-31 (March 1983).

NOTE: The ratio will equal one if the U.S. and foreign prices are equal.

a.   Canada No. 1 Western red spring 13.5% protein wheat, in store Thunder Bay; U.S. No. 2 hard winter ordinary protein wheat, f.o.b. Gulf ports.

b.   Argentina, f.o.b. Buenos Aires; U.S. No. 2 yellow, f.o.b. Gulf ports.

large stocks and no PIK-like programs would be more compatible with a strategic stance in trade negotiations.

Direction and Scope

Secretary Block's unstated goal was the improvement of farm prices and income. This is the traditional goal of secretaries of agriculture; but it is a difficult one to defend from the standpoint of the nation as a whole. The Executive Office of the President (including the Office of Management and Budget and other White House branches) has typically taken a broader view, understanding that the political methods employed to improve farm income work only by reducing someone else's income. Consequently, there is often tension between the White House staff and the Department of Agriculture.

President Carter was said to be interested in details, and his attempts to manage U.S. agriculture fit this image. The best example was the Farmer-Owned Reserve (FOR) program, which attempted to establish two, three, or even four different trigger prices for each grain; each trigger had its own function in regulating production incentives, market prices, or the accumulation or release of stocks nominally owned by farmers. The Carter administration seemed to view the USDA as a control center for the commodity markets, where signals from the marketplace would be rationalized by the adjustment of various policy levers to correct the market's deviations from course. The FOR program did contribute to price stability by increasing stocks, but this could have been done just as effectively, much more simply.[27] The Reagan USDA retained the program but reduced its scope and simplified the price triggers.

President Reagan's more relaxed, chairman-of-the-board style creates different problems. By law USDA is now the manager of the main U.S. farm commodity markets, but the administration's policy preference is to let them manage themselves. Under PIK, the details of administration are of unprecedented complexity and difficulty, and the government may pay insufficient attention to them. The PIK program amounts to a revival of the New Deal in agriculture, and there will be new tensions between USDA and the White House as PIK's inevitable administrative problems and allocative inefficiencies appear.

Beyond farm commodity policy, there exist other agricultural policy issues including food safety and nutrition, marketing regulation, rural development, and agricultural research and information dissemination. Carter gave consumer interests a new visibility by appointing Carol Foreman, formerly with the Consumer Federation of America, as an assistant secretary. The substantive changes toward more regulatory activism—notably attempts to regulate the marketing of mechanically deboned meat products as well as the addition of nitrites to bacon—engendered intense lobbying and judicial struggles, and ended with only labeling requirements. More substantive innovations in agricultural policy were the establishment of the Commodity Futures Trading Commission and the Federal Grain Inspection Service during the Ford administration. Nonetheless, over time traditional farm interests have seen their influence waning in "their" department,[28] and the Reagan administration has responded by appointing a more traditional farmer-oriented staff at the Department of Agriculture.

The real economic impact of the changed emphasis at USDA has not been measured, but it is probably slight. In terms of budget authority, comparison of Carter's fiscal year 1980 and 1981 as compared with Reagan's

---

27. Grounds for this assertion are contained in B. Gardner, "Consequences of USDA's Farmer-Owned Reserve Program," U.S. General Accounting Office, CED-81-70 (June 1981). In its first three years the FOR program was probably quite inefficient in adding to stocks, with only one additional bushel of carryover for each four in the FOR. The reason is that three bushels left non-FOR private speculative stocks as the prospects for the profitable disposal diminished. But in its fourth and fifth years the FOR program seems to have had a substantially larger effect, perhaps one additional bushel of total stocks for two in the FOR program. See L. Salathe, D. Banker, and J. Price, "The Impacts of the Farm-Owned Reserve . . .," Mimeo, USDA-ERS, 1983.

28. See John Kramer, "Agriculture's Role in Government Decisions," in B. Gardner and J. Richardson, eds., *Consensus and Conflict in U.S. Agriculture* (College Station, Texas: Texas A & M University Press, 1979) pp. 207–241.

requests for fiscal year 1984, shows that funding for the Food Safety and Inspection Service is down 5 percent, for the Federal Grain Inspection Service it is down 70 percent, for the Food and Nutrition Service (including Food Stamps) it is up 15 percent, for the Rural Electrification Administration it is down 38 percent, and for the Soil Conservation Service it is down 10 percent. The agricultural research budget (including federal research funds at universities) is up 22 percent; the Animal and Plant Inspection Service budget is down 10 percent, and the sum of all these programs is up 13 percent, to $17.7 billion (primarily because the Food Stamp program dwarfs the others).

Rural development, encompassing programs to aid rural people through a variety of means besides commodity policy, received less attention in the 1970s than in previous decades. During the Carter administration there were some changes in direction, notably in providing subsidized credit to rural residents on an emergency or disaster basis. New programs, such as the Emergency Feed Program and the Disaster Payments Program, were closely tied to commercial agriculture. These programs have been substantially reduced, but this does not necessarily show a strong difference between the Carter and Reagan administrations; the Disaster Program was largely eliminated by the Agriculture and Food Act of 1981.

One area in which Reagan's cutbacks are questionable is the funding for economic statistics related to agriculture. In March 1982, the Statistical Reporting Service (SRS) of the Department of Agriculture, responding to a 25 percent budget cut since 1980, eliminated 26 agricultural reports and the surveys on which they were based. The SRS Farm Labor survey had earlier been cut from four times per year to once, greatly reducing its value because of the seasonal nature of farm labor patterns.[29]

Summary

A basic criticism of current agriculture policy is that support prices are too high for grains, cotton, and milk—"too high" in the sense that they cause large deadweight losses, or real resource costs that generate no compensating gains to anyone. For example, even the best possible management of commodities, under the constraints of the 1981 Agriculture and Food Act, would involve a deadweight loss in the corn program that would amount to about $2 billion in 1983. According to admittedly rough estimates, the ad-

---

29. Details of these cuts are described and evaluated in Gardner, "Fact and Fiction in the Public Data Budget Crunch," *American Journal of Agricultural Economics* (December 1983).

ministration's PIK policy involved an expected deadweight loss of about $3 billion for corn alone; but the main criticism must be leveled at Congress for placing the support prices so high. (Although a detailed analysis of the programs for the other grains and cotton was not provided here, conditions are roughly the same. But because corn is by far the most important cash crop, the other grain and cotton programs combined would only roughly double the deadweight loss figures for corn.)

The dairy program is even more out of balance in relative terms, and again the main problem is the congressionally mandated support price. Other problems include the commodity policies for sugar, peanuts, and tobacco, as well as marketing orders. In all these areas the Reagan administration has signaled that it would like to pursue reforms that appear quite sensible. The administration may be criticized for not pressing sufficiently for reforms in policy governing sugar and peanuts, and for too readily acquiescing in USDA support for marketing orders that regulate the flow to market of citrus products and some other commodities and the classified pricing of milk. While the administration's major mistaken policy is PIK, that program did show the administration's willingness to try fairly large-scale reforms in policy. It might be a springboard to even more adventuresome policy actions—deregulation of some of the commodity prices, for example.

Serious moves toward such deregulation would be feasible only if substitute programs are devised to moderate the instabilities of farm prices and incomes. In this respect the administration's role in legalizing experiments in trading commodity options is promising. The availability of "put" options for corn and other commodities, for example, would enable farmers to buy price protection of the kind that target prices now provide, with no cost to the taxpayer and fewer resource-allocation distortions. The feasibility of such an approach is far from certain, but the idea should be explored.

On the other hand, the administration seems too eager to repudiate the idea, emphasized by the Carter administration, promoting the carrying of stocks for price stabilization; and although the administration's cutbacks in some noncommodity agricultural programs have reduced waste, there have also been cutbacks (such as the drop in funding for agricultural statistics) that were mistaken from a public interest viewpoint.

In summary, the Reagan administration inherited a set of agricultural programs that had largely outlived what usefulness they may once have had, and had to contend with a Congress intent on overspending on farm policy. The Reagan administration has declared intentions, as have previous administrations, to modernize and rationalize the governmental role in agriculture. To date it has been unsuccessful, and the innovations successfully introduced have been of questionable value.

ABOUT THE AUTHORS

Robert W. Crandall is a senior fellow at The Brookings Institution where he specializes in the economics of regulation, industrial organization, and antitrust policy. His publications include *The Steel Industry in Recurrent Crisis, Controlling Industrial Pollution,* and *The Scientific Basis of Health and Safety Regulation* (with L. Lave). Prior to joining Brookings in 1978, he was deputy director of the U.S. Council on Wage and Price Stability. From 1966 through 1974 he taught economics at the Massachusetts Institute of Technology. He has also taught at Northwestern University, George Washington University, and the University of Maryland.

Bruce Gardner is a professor in the Department of Agricultural and Resource Economics at the University of Maryland. His recent research has involved estimating the consequences and explaining the causes of U.S. agricultural policy. His published work in this area includes two books: *Optimal Stockpiling of Grain* and *The Governing of Agriculture,* as well as many articles on particular policy issues.

William W. Hogan, professor of political economy, serves as chairman of the Public Policy Program and director of the Energy and Environmental Policy Center at Harvard. His interests are in the theory and application of analytic methods for public policy. He has held positions dealing with energy policy analysis in the Federal Energy Administration, including deputy assistant administrator for data and analysis.

John D. Leshy has been professor of law at Arizona State University College of Law since 1980. He teaches constitutional law, water law, Indian law, and public land/natural resources law. He writes and consults mainly in the area of natural resources management and protection. A graduate of Harvard College and Harvard Law School, Mr. Leshy previously worked at the Department of Justice, the Natural Resources Defense Council, and the Department of the Interior, where he served as associate solicitor for energy and resources under Cecil Andrus.

Paul R. Portney is a senior fellow at Resources for the Future. His recent research has been concerned with the effects of air pollutants and other environmental hazards on health, and with the reform of environmental regulation. He is the editor of *Current Issues in U.S. Environmental Policy*. Dr. Portney previously served as visiting professor at the University of California at Berkeley and as senior staff economist at the White House Council on Environmental Quality.

PARTICIPANTS

Cathy Abbott
*Interstate Natural Gas
Association of America*

John Andelin
U.S. Congress

James Blum
Congressional Budget Office

David Bodde
Congressional Budget Office

Daniel Boggs
Office of Policy Development

Sterling Brubaker
Resources for the Future

Ann Brunsdale
American Enterprise Institute

Joseph Cannon
Environmental Protection Agency

Edwin C. Clark
The Conservation Foundation

Bill Davis
Department of Energy

Robert K. Davis
Department of the Interior

Everett Ehrlich
Congressional Budget Office

Dennis Ellerman
National Coal Association

Arthur Fraas
OIRA

Ken Frederick
Resources for the Future

Katherine Gillman
Independent Consultant

Susan Greene
Resources for the Future

Winston Harrington
Resources for the Future

Robert Healy
The Conservation Foundation

Barbara Huddleston
*International Ford Policy
Research Institute*

Caroline Isber
Save EPA

Allen Kneese
Resources for the Future

Trish Knight
Department of Energy

Edwin K. Law
U.S. Congress

Richard Liroff
The Conservation Foundation

Joan M. McGovern
League of Women Voters'
Educational Fund

James MacKenzie
Union of Concerned Scientists

Dave Montgomery
Resources for the Future

Richard Morgenstern
Environmental Protection Agency

Richard Morrison
National Science Foundation

Andy Morton
Congressional Budget Office

John Mullahy
Resources for the Future

Pat Parentou
National Wildlife Federation

William Quandt
The Brookings Institution

Lawrence Rosenberg
National Science Foundation

Neil Schaller
U.S. Department of Agriculture

Jack Schanz
Congressional Research Service

Jack Silvey
Office of Policy, Planning and
Analysis

Miron Straf
National Academy of Sciences

Richard Styrup
Department of the Interior

Glen Sweetnam
Department of Energy

William Taylor
U.S. Congress

Myron Uman
National Academy of Sciences

Ben Weekly
Department of Energy